COSMIC

NUMEROLOGY

HOW TO HARNESS YOUR FULL POTENTIAL
USING THE POWER OF NUMBERS AND PLANETS

JENN KING

NUMBERS
+
PLANETS

WISDOM
+
SELF-
KNOWLEDGE

A
MYSTICAL
UNION

Numbers are a universal language that help us make sense of our seemingly chaotic world. Each single-digit number from 1 to 9 is said to hold its own specific energy, vibration or power within. Numerology is mystical mathematics, decoding the meaning of these numbers and assigning special significance to them. Some traditions work with numbers alone, while others also assign numerical value to letters. No particular belief system is necessary to explore the mysteries of numerology – it is as universal as numbers themselves. Humankind has followed this rich and multifaceted tradition since the times of ancient civilisations in Egypt, Babylon, Greece, Rome, Scandinavia, India, China and Japan. Symbolic numbers have frequented fairytales, myths, religious texts, stories, superstitions and other cultural folklore through the ages.

Ever since I can remember, numbers and planets have exerted a powerful gravitational pull on me. I inherited a love of numbers from my father, and my curiosity has led me to seek knowledge of their mysteries throughout my life. As a teenager and adult, I've studied numerology, astrology, tarot, meditation, yoga and all things mystical. Over years of building up a body of knowledge, as various teachings collided, it became clear to me how the numbers and planets fitted together. In astrology, planets loom large in importance – information about this is easily found – but how the planets also relate to numbers is often overlooked. The intersection of numbers and planets makes perfect sense, as the properties attributed to planets mirror the properties attributed to numbers. They are forever married in a mystical union, their kinship obvious.

While all numerology systems focus on numbers, cosmic numerology connects the numbers to their companion planets. I hope, through bringing together the languages of numerology and astrology in my own particular way, that new perspectives and deeper levels of understanding can unfold for you. In this book, the focus is firmly on the day and numbers of your date

7

of birth and their planetary associations. The day and date you were born cannot ever be altered and are positioned at the very core of who you are. From your birth date, your foundation, personality and destiny numbers and planets can be discovered. They act like a blueprint of your personality, highlighting your strengths, talents and gifts and providing you with clues as to which paths might be beneficial to follow and which unsuitable moulds you should never try to squeeze yourself into. By making the best of what you were born with, learning the meanings of your numbers and planets, and working with this knowledge, you will be better able to understand yourself, others and the world around you.

LUCKY AND UNLUCKY NUMBERS

✦✦✦

Superstitions about numbers are very common. Many people fear certain numbers, or believe some to be lucky. Ask anyone about their favourite or least-liked numbers and they will usually be able to tell you immediately. They may or may not know *why* they feel this way, but feel it they do. Sometimes these beliefs are the result of social conditioning; sometimes they're instinctive. In many cultures there exists – or existed – the idea that some numbers are special, either in the positive or negative sense. Ancient Egyptians especially loved 3 and 7; to them, 3 represented plurality and 7 perfection. The Norse favoured 3 and 9: there are 3 roots at the base of Yggdrasil (the sacred ash tree) and 9 worlds supported by the tree. The Celts revered 3 as representing the triple deity and 5 for the elements of life, while the Chinese consider 8 the number of wealth and 4 the number of death.

No number is as maligned as 13, which becomes the single-digit number 4 when you add 1 + 3. Many hotels and buildings have no thirteenth floor, or thirteenth room; some aeroplanes and trains even have no seat thirteen. Triskaidekaphobia, the phobia of 13, and tetraphobia, the phobia of 4, are extreme versions of the fear of these numbers. The death card is number 13 in the tarot deck and this is no coincidence. Numbers 4 and 13 are ruled by Uranus, the planet of upheaval, revolution and alchemy. Personally, I believe 13 is wrongly maligned. People are often afraid of change, assuming it will always be difficult or to their detriment, and that's why they reject 13. Our reaction to the transformational nature of 13 says more about us than it does about the number. All changes bring their own deaths, but carried along with each death is a major blessing: rebirth.

The year 2020 was a perfect example of number 4 energy in motion. The year was dominated by a pandemic and society went through huge economic change and complete disruption to our so-called 'normal life'. Conspiracy theories exploded and there was mass death, civil unrest, natural disasters, protests galore and plenty of political upheaval. The flipside was that people began to question the status quo and carbon emissions were drastically reduced during lockdowns.

Incredible scientific discoveries and inventions forged ahead, including new vaccines, the further development of plastic-eating enzymes, the presence of water confirmed on Mars, even a new type of T cell receptor in our blood that might be a potential universal cancer treatment. 'Sustainable' became the ideal consumer scenario, with cow-free dairy, recycled fabrics, lab-grown meat and carbon-negative vodka 'made out of air' being just a few examples of brilliant, revolutionary 'mad inventor' Uranus and number 4–style thinking.

There are times in your life when you'll come across repetitive numbers, such as 888, 1111, 555 ... When this happens, I believe it is the number speaking to you in an amplified way and wanting to draw your attention to its specific qualities.

Some numerologists associate these numbers with angelic presences, and others call them messages from your spirit guides. Many people believe that each number, when repeated, has a specific meaning attached. The important thing, though, is that when you notice these repetitive numbers, ask yourself what the message is and listen to your intuition for the answer.

Have you ever had a special feeling about a particular number, or the sense that a certain number doesn't quite gel? That's because numbers carry specific energy that will feel either comfortable or challenging for you. I've always favoured the number 8. I was born on the eighth and feel a natural affinity for it. This book was accepted for publishing on the eighth, which made me extra happy. There's just something about the way there is no beginning and no end to the shape of 8 that I find comforting. I was obsessed with the concept of infinity as a child, and it wasn't until my teenage years that I discovered 8 symbolises infinity. Meanwhile, 7 makes me uncomfortable, maybe because to me it feels uncertain, wishy washy and, on a subconscious level, unclear. I had an extraordinarily difficult and confusing period of my life in a number 7 house (based on the street number) which, strangely, I lived in for seven years. Although the deep healing and insight gained from that time has been valuable, I am much more at ease in my 5 place and life feels effortless in comparison. I am now learning to love 7 and focus on its beautiful mystical, creative and dreamy qualities.

Challenges present us with opportunities to learn and grow. The trick is to understand the meanings behind numbers and learn to collaborate with them so that you can work their specific blessings into your life. It is disempowering and unhelpful to assign good or bad status to a number. Polarities are everywhere in the world, and both beneficial and difficult aspects exist for each number, like almost everything in life. The more awareness you have of this, the better able you will be to bring out the best in the numbers you encounter.

WHAT IS COSMIC NUMEROLOGY?

✦✦✦

People have always looked to the planets for guidance, inspiration and wisdom. The classic maxim of mysticism, 'as above, so below', illustrates this connection perfectly. What is up above us, out there in space, exerts influence over us here on Earth. For millennia, reverence and curiosity have kept us seeking more knowledge of the skies above. We want to know the unknown and see the unseen. This is why we have a desire to understand the planets on a philosophical and metaphysical level.

Cosmic numerology is numerology with an extra dimension. In astrology, the planets are referred to as being the driving forces behind each sign, but did you know that numbers and the days of the week also have their own planetary influences? Each day and each number has a ruling planet, unique expression and archetypal energy – this system unites them. Cosmic numerology is like the lovechild of numerology and astrology, the amalgamation of what I have learned about numbers and planets over the years. By incorporating planetary intelligence into numerology, extra magic and support is accessible.

Many scholars from different periods of time have contributed to our current body of knowledge about planets, since we first began looking to the skies for guidance and weaving this wisdom into our mythologies. Influential planetary thinking comes from Pythagoras (born 570 BCE), who believed each planet had its own sound, Persian astrologer Abu Ma'shar (born 787 CE) and English astrologer William Lilly (born 1602 CE). Modern-day sages include Scott Cunningham, who documented magical planetary associations, the numerologists Cheiro and Sepharial, and Universal Kabbalist Dr Joseph Michael Levry, all of whom discuss numbers and their planetary influences in their works.

The mythology of planets is a living thing, continuously evolving and creating opportunities for us to discover more about the universe and ourselves in the below zone. The influence of the planets, even at a cultural level, is huge. Astrology is one of the more well-known planetary practices, but many other traditions hold the belief that the planets have special powers – Indigenous Australians, Native Americans and most other First Nations cultures attach specific attributes to the planets, as did the Ancient Romans, Greeks, Anglo-Saxons, Vikings, Celts and Egyptians. To this day, all over the world, many people have beliefs about planets and their energies, and assign great significance to them.

In cosmic numerology, a number is associated with each of the seven classical planets, which are the seven moving planets (or astronomical bodies, in the case of the Sun and Moon) visible to the naked eye. These are the Sun, the Moon, Mars, Mercury, Jupiter, Venus and Saturn. But, of course, there are nine single-digit numbers in numerology. The other two planets that bring us to nine are Uranus and Neptune. These are considered the 'shadow' or 'unseen' planets that influence our lives and are rarely (Uranus) or never (Neptune) visible to the naked eye from Earth. They might be unseen, but they still have huge amounts of power. Uranus and Neptune are thought to be extra spiritually charged and are often assigned the numbers 4 and 7 in modern times.

The exact origins of connecting numbers to planets is difficult to trace, as it has such a long history. In classical numerology traditions, which date back to around 500 BCE, planets were attributed to particular numbers because they were thought to express the same aspects. But instead of assigning Uranus to number 4 and Neptune to number 7, these early systems often assigned different entities. Rahu and Ketu, the nodes of the moon, are used in Vedic astrology and numerology traditions, while in Western traditions it was common to assign either the Sun or Earth to 4 and the Moon or full Moon to 7. It is a more modern system of astrology and numerology that brings in Uranus and Neptune – they began to be incorporated after their discovery in the eighteenth and nineteenth centuries. In addition to their affinity with a particular number, all of the nine celestial bodies have their own specific rapport with certain parts and systems of the human body, healing plants, essential oils and colours. They also govern the twelve zodiac signs of astrology and the days of our week.

HOW TO USE THIS BOOK

✦✦✦

The numbers and planets derived from your date of birth are the main archetypal energies present within you and at work in your life. Remember, there are no purely negative or positive numbers and planets. Each placement has its challenges and blessings. You can work with this book to discover deeper levels of self-knowledge, access your talents, bring awareness to your strengths and balance out your challenging aspects. You can also use it to check out your relationships and discover other people's numbers and planets. By doing so, you will be better able to enhance your connections and avoid conflict. Always use numerology for good.

Each chapter also provides information on which colours, days of the week, elements, astrological signs, tarot cards, body zones, herbs and essential oils relate to a particular planet. These kindred associates are accessible to anyone who wants to connect with a planet's energies, even if you don't have that planet as one of your numerology placements. Explore them in a way that suits you. Specialised meditations and suggestions as to how you can balance the planet's influence, be inspired by it and access its magic are also included. So, for example, if you are a gentle Moon person who is feeling unmotivated and might like a bit of fire in your mix, you could look up the Mars kindred associates and find ways to bring some of that dynamic Mars energy into your world.

The main aim of this book is to share this information in a way that doesn't require specialist skills or knowledge to decode.

There are only nine numbers and planets to learn about. You don't need to understand complex birth charts or memorise intricate systems, as with astrology or the tarot deck.

This is deep spiritual information, simplified to enhance your everyday life.

A NOTE ON ESSENTIAL OILS
AND HEALING HERBS

✦✦✦

As a herbalist and aromatherapist, I regularly assist my numerology clients in selecting essential oils and herbs. Caution must be applied regarding use of the oils and herbs listed in the kindred planet associates sections.

This information is not intended to replace personalised professional advice on health care and wellbeing. It is not intended to be used to diagnose or treat.

The herbs listed are meant to be taken in tea form, not in excess of one cup a day, or sprinkled in small amounts on food as a seasoning. Consult a qualified herbalist if you would like to use herbal medicine for a specific issue. If you have medical conditions or take medications, check with your health practitioner and herbalist before taking herbs, as some may interact negatively. If you have allergies to any plant families, avoid herbs from those families. If in doubt, don't ingest.

Essential oils must be diluted before applying to the skin. The maximum dose is twelve drops per 20 millilitres, which is a 3 per cent dilution. Use a 1 per cent dilution of four drops per 20 millilitres if you have sensitive skin (you still receive the benefits in low quantities: essential oils are very strong). Never use them on your face or sensitive areas. Never use them on children, and avoid diffusing or burning them around children under two years old, unless advised by a qualified aromatherapist. Only use mild oils in the bath at a maximum of three drops. Essential oils should not be ingested: they are recommended for inhalation and external use only. Always do a patch test. Only buy dried herbs and essential oils from reputable and ethical sources or registered practitioners, and be sure to select only the medicinal varieties.

HOW TO DO A NUMEROLOGY CALCULATION

In numerology, the single-digit numbers from 1 to 9 are conceptually assigned their own particular meanings, planetary rulers and other affinities, potentials, challenges and relationships. They are thought to be extra potent, because they cannot be further 'reduced'. Any number, no matter how lengthy, can be reduced to a single-digit number between 1 and 9 using fadic addition: adding numbers together until you are left with a single digit. The below example reduces my date of birth. I'm Australian, so the date is written in the 'day, month, year' format – but the numerology calculations work the same no matter how you write dates in your part of the world.

FADIC ADDITION

EXAMPLE

8 MAY 1979

$$8 + 5 + 1 + 9 + 7 + 9 = 39$$
$$3 + 9 = 12$$
$$1 + 2 = 3$$

This book focuses on four key cosmic numerology calculations: the foundation, personality, destiny and relationship numbers. Some of these areas – such as the destiny (or life path) number and the day of the week you were born – are universal building blocks throughout astrology and numerology traditions; cosmic numerology unites the wisdom of both systems and unlocks new levels of understanding. Read on to learn how to calculate each of these significant life numbers and find out their corresponding planets.

THE DAYS OF THE WEEK

AND THEIR RULING PLANETS

✦✦✦

DAY OF THE WEEK	PLANETARY RULER
Sunday	Sun
Monday	Moon
Tuesday	Mars
Wednesday	Mercury
Thursday	Jupiter
Friday	Venus
Saturday	Saturn

THE NUMBERS

AND THEIR RULING PLANETS

✦✦✦

NUMBER	PLANETARY RULER
1	Sun
2	Moon
3	Jupiter
4	Uranus
5	Mercury
6	Venus
7	Neptune
8	Saturn
9	Mars

FOUNDATION NUMBER AND PLANET

Your foundation number and planet are based on the weekday on which you were born. This placement is significant because the days of the week have long been assigned planets, deities and other special properties in many cultures. Your particular weekday represents your foundation, which is what you are greeting the world with and what the world greeted you with when you entered this life. This placement is like your Sun sign in astrology: it is the main underlying structure that supports your other aspects. If life is like a theatre, then the foundation placement is the lead role, while the personality number plays the supporting role.

If you don't already know the day of the week you were born, it should be easy to find an online calendar for your year of birth. Use the charts on the previous page or the list below to find out which planet was in power on this day, along with its corresponding number.

DAY OF THE WEEK YOU WERE BORN

EXAMPLES
8 MAY 1979 = TUESDAY
TUESDAY = MARS

MARS = 9

27 OCTOBER 1999 = WEDNESDAY
WEDNESDAY = MERCURY

MERCURY = 5

SUNDAY = SUN | MONDAY = MOON | TUESDAY = MARS | WEDNESDAY = MERCURY |
THURSDAY = JUPITER | FRIDAY = VENUS | SATURDAY = SATURN

1 = SUN | 2 = MOON | 3 = JUPITER | 4 = URANUS | 5 = MERCURY | 6 = VENUS
7 = NEPTUNE | 8 = SATURN | 9 = MARS

PERSONALITY NUMBER AND PLANET

Your personality number (also known as your birthday number) and planet are derived from the day of the month you were born. This placement is all about the influence on your personality, which is shown in the way you think, perceive, process and express yourself in relation to the world around you and in connection to others in your sphere. Think of it as the constant narrative that runs through your behaviour, thoughts and emotions. This placement projects from you in the way you speak and interact with other people and your environment, as well as in your internal dialogue.

To find out your personality number and planet, all you need is the day of the month of your birthday. If it is a two-digit number, add the numbers together until you have a single-digit number. This is your personality number. Use the chart on pages 18–19 or the list below to find out which planet rules this number.

DAY OF THE MONTH YOU WERE BORN

EXAMPLES
8 MAY = 8

8 = SATURN

27 OCTOBER = 27
2 + 7 = 9

9 = MARS

1 = SUN | 2 = MOON | 3 = JUPITER | 4 = URANUS | 5 = MERCURY | 6 = VENUS
7 = NEPTUNE | 8 = SATURN | 9 = MARS

DESTINY NUMBER AND PLANET

The destiny number encompasses who you become as you move through life. The destiny placement indicates your potential expression as much as it does your deeper nature and what shapes you. This is your most spiritually rich placement. As you mature, your destiny can be the source of your greatest happiness when you lean into it. Your destiny number and planet are guides to where your talents and innate gifts lie. This placement also shows aspects of the self that develop through interaction with life and become more embedded with time. The destiny number is sometimes referred to as the life path number. When you make good use of your capabilities, you fulfil your life path and align with who you are destined to be. Having said that, it's not a fate trap that has you locked in to being a certain way; it is a doorway to fulfilment and an opportunity to experience self-actualisation. Remember, nurture trumps nature. You *can* co-create.

Your destiny number and planet are derived from all the numbers of your date of birth added to make a single-digit number, using fadic addition. Use the chart on pages 18–19 or the list below to find out which planet rules this number.

BIRTH DAY + MONTH + YEAR

EXAMPLE

8 MAY 1979

$8 + 5 + 1 + 9 + 7 + 9 = 39$

$3 + 9 = 12$

$1 + 2 = 3$

3 = JUPITER

1 = SUN | 2 = MOON | 3 = JUPITER | 4 = URANUS | 5 = MERCURY | 6 = VENUS
7 = NEPTUNE | 8 = SATURN | 9 = MARS

RELATIONSHIIP NUMBER AND PLANET

W hen you bring two people together, you create a third entity: the relationship. A relationship has its own life and is greater than the sum of its parts. This applies to all the different kinds of personal relationships, not only the romantic ones. In a partnership, family relationship, friendship or other connection, you are moving forwards in life together and this is constantly unfolding, never fixed.

To calculate a relationship number, we use the destiny numbers of the two people, as they contain the energies of both full birth dates. The combined destinies give an overall destiny number for the relationship. As a mirror to the individual destiny numbers, this combination shares the deeper natures and highest potentials of the pair. Like every other placement, the relationship number and planet have beneficial and challenging aspects, gifts and lessons. Remember to look at this as a gateway to help you bring out the best in yourself and the relationship, so that this connection can fulfil its brightest destiny, whether it lasts a short time or a lifetime.

To discover the number and planet of any relationship, add the destiny numbers of the two people (learn how to calculate a destiny number on page 23) and use fadic addition to reach a single digit. Use the chart on pages 18–19 or the list below to find out which planet rules this number.

YOUR DESTINY NUMBER + THEIR DESTINY NUMBER

EXAMPLE

6 + 9 = 15

1 + 5 = 6

6 = VENUS

1 = SUN | 2 = MOON | 3 = JUPITER | 4 = URANUS | 5 = MERCURY | 6 = VENUS
7 = NEPTUNE | 8 = SATURN | 9 = MARS

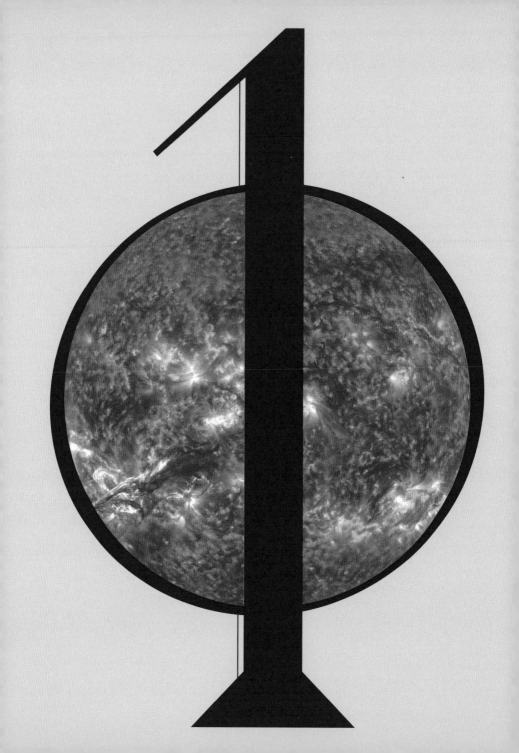

SUN

MAGNANIMOUS ✦ **RADIANT** ✦ *BRIGHT*

THE NUMBER 1

♦♦♦

The number 1 is the first of the nine single-digit numbers. This number is at the beginning of it all – when you add 1 to any number, you get the next number. In this way, 1 has a highly creative energy: it makes things greater. Without 1, there is no other number. The number 1 is singular and standalone in its energy, and expresses individuality. This number represents the sense of a higher power and is connected to the energy of the supreme consciousness, divine creator or god archetype.

The dynamic of this number is very much about the self, and how it relates to the world outside. Those with 1 in their chart are considered to be self-concerned, but also concerned with the self as perceived by others. The number 1 carries a lot of energy with it and has a driven and ambitious vibe. It's not a coincidence that the figure on tarot card number 1, the Magician, is directing their will and personal power outwards with the aim of realising their intentions and reaching their fullest potential. The number 1 provides us with the confidence to go for what we want in life. It encourages us to focus our energy and willpower on self-actualisation and achieving our ambitions.

The number of leadership, 1 teaches us about stepping up and stepping out, and putting ourselves on the line in pursuit of what we want. It can give us a bit of a one-track mind and make us a little self-absorbed, so its lesson is in sharing. Looking beyond our personal desires and giving something of ourselves or our blessings to the greater good is where the energies of 1 can be beneficial. Although 1 is self-sufficient and rooted in its independence, there is also need for external connection and somewhere to belong – or another to belong with.

THE SUN

The Sun shines on everyone, regardless of who they are. From those of the lowest social standing to the highest of the high, from healthiest to sickest, kindest to nastiest, richest to poorest … none of it matters to the Sun. This brightest star gives its warmth and light to everyone on Earth; without it, there would be no life. Its generosity of spirit is a great lesson to us all.

The Sun was considered a planet by the ancients; however, technically the Sun is a star. It's our biggest and brightest star, sitting at the centre of our solar system. Everything revolves around the Sun, which is where its associations with beginning, coming first, the self, ego, ambition, a willingness to lead and a desire for attention originate. The Sun is the spirit that animates all; for us, this is reflected as the soul behind the ego, the great spark within us that is believed to transcend life and death. We associate vitality and life force with the Sun, too: without its energy, our solar system would be lifeless. We literally cannot exist in its absence. No wonder so many civilisations – Egyptians, Aztecs, Sumerians, Romans, Norse, to name a few – have either worshipped the Sun directly, or a deity version of it.

The energetic aspects of the Sun are active, stimulating, drying and warming. The star itself is a giant ball of burning plasma and gas, whose gravity and magnetic field hold the entire solar system in its embrace. The energy of the Sun influences our oceans, weather systems, seasonal changes and climate. There are many versions of the word 'Sun' in Anglo and Germanic languages, with people often also connecting the Roman god Sol (the personification of the Sun) to the name.

This star is so important to our corner of the universe that everything within its reach, from the most massive planet to the tiniest piece of space debris, is part of its friendship circle. The Sun is the head of our solar system family.

1

✦

SUN
FOUNDATION

◆————————————————◆

DAY
OF THE
WEEK
**YOU
WERE
BORN**
=
SUNDAY

Sun foundation people are bright sparks. You have an ingrained ability to light up a room when you enter, and your warm nature is hugely attractive and magnetic to other people. You are a friend to all and usually have a lot of people circling around you. The Sun does secretly want to have everything revolve around it – this feels like the natural order of things. That doesn't necessarily mean you have a huge ego (although this can sometimes be the case); it's more that you are drawn to situations requiring a leader, guiding light, anchor point, or star of the show.

This planet in this placement is the one most likely to create fame for a person. This can manifest in a variety of ways, from the double-edged sword of celebrity and notoriety, to being a leading person in your chosen field or head of an organisation, company or other entity. Either way, the Sun doesn't go unnoticed. In fact, in all areas of your life – from work to family to romance – you need to be recognised and rewarded for all that you give. It's highly important that you are seen and appreciated, as you really do care what other people think of you and how you are perceived. This can be a real source of anguish if you are surrounded by unappreciative types or people who never express gratitude.

Self-esteem is an area that needs a lot of nurturing when the Sun is your foundation. It's vital that you nourish your sense of self through your actions and through connecting with what pleases you in life, rather than seeking it from external validation. You can never be truly happy within yourself if you rely on feedback and attention from others to prop you up. Sun people have the ability to achieve a lot and go far in their lives – they are highly ambitious and love to do well. Success is inevitable when a Sun focuses their brightness and strong will on a goal. Make sure that the dreams you are chasing are truly your own and remember to live your life for you.

Being solid for your close allies and loved ones and always ready to cheer other people up makes you a great friend, partner and colleague. Your presence is light yet powerful and you have the gift of lifting and boosting other people, coaxing them out of their shells and drawing out their best efforts. Sun foundations make excellent bosses, heads of departments and team captains: they are great go-getters with lots of enthusiasm and a can-do positive attitude. Do make sure you let others have their turn in the limelight, by encouraging them to step forward. Everyone loves the Sun and this energy makes a person easy to love, too. Shine on those around you, guide them from the heart and enjoy watching them flourish.

Sun foundations have a charitable nature with plenty of compassion and a love of giving. Being of service to the world means a lot to you, and you have plenty of goodness to share. This might be personal – between you and another person you help or mentor – or something you do to benefit a larger cause. Generosity is a very Sun characteristic and you can't abide tight-fisted or closed-hearted people. Find those with big hearts to share yours with and you won't go wrong. You believe life is to be enjoyed, and you are right; don't hold yourself back or hide your light away. You are meant to radiate your energy outwards, be a big presence in the world and make an impact.

At the centre of the action is where Sun foundation people can be found. You have strong energy and long to be part of the happenings around you. Yes, you like attention but it's often more about wanting to be included, to be a part of things. You prefer to get involved, dive in and get your hands dirty, rather than sit idly on the sidelines. Even better, if you get to the forefront, to lead the way. Suns can be a touch egoistic, in the sense that they want to be the best and brightest in any group. Enjoy your achievements and let yourself bask in them before moving on to the next thing. Always stay humble, no matter how far you go in life.

To bring out the best of your Sun foundation, it's important to appreciate yourself, appreciate others and make sure you receive appreciation, too. Don't let fear of how you might be viewed, or outdated material markers of success, stand in the way of putting yourself, your gifts and your work out there. Work on caring less about what other people think of you and on enjoying the freedom that comes from living solely for your own approval. You have a greater chance of achieving what you want when you allow yourself to fully express your talents and shine as brightly as you can. Believe in yourself: put your big energy behind the projects, aspirations and dreams that make your heart sing. Have courage and reveal your true self. Allow yourself to give, feel, receive and share all the love. Always obey the impulse you have towards kindness and compassion.

1

✦

SUN
PERSONALITY

✦————————————————✦

DAY
OF THE
MONTH
YOU
WERE
BORN

=

1

The Sun in this placement gives you a beginner's mind. The Sun personality is not afraid to learn new things and see the world with fresh eyes, rather than letting worn-out assumptions get in the way. You like to live in the present and not be dragged down by the past. Being alive on this planet can be tough, but you have a zest for life and a happy-go-lucky attitude that bounces away negativity like a shiny suit of optimistic armour. Sun personalities love to make the most of everything and prefer hanging around and interacting with other upbeat people. After all, isn't enjoying the ride half the fun of living?

Sun people have masses of presence. You exude personal power and have a very strong and determined personality (some might say stubborn and intense). You are very much an individual and prefer plenty of free rein to do your own thing. Despite the fact that you have a self-contained and self-governing way of being, you do deeply love the people of your inner circle and will do your best to support and care for them. The Sun personality has a very driven nature, with plenty of ambition. You might not mention it often, but you are secretly always working towards bettering yourself and realising your dreams.

The Sun personality is what I call the hidden Sun. Those with this placement can hide their ambitions, even stifling their own growth out of fear of not being good enough. This can lead to self-sabotage: you might have had times when you've subconsciously trodden on the flowers of your dreams just in case you're not up to the task of tending them. You might sometimes feel self-doubt and will need to work on cultivating self-belief, so that you can experience the fullness of who you are. Don't beat yourself up if something doesn't work out – neither you, nor anything in life, is meant to be perfect. Trust that the right thing is just around the corner and you have everything you need within you to make the most of it.

Your power or clout might not be obvious or known – Sun personalities are often the quiet leaders. You are as likely to be the person steering the ship from the back as the one at the front. You can switch your magnetism on and off, though, and be very charismatic when the situation calls for it. You might be the figurehead onto which other people project their version of you, and this can sometimes make you feel separate from others. Because you are so determined to achieve your personal best in everything you do, it can be lonely at the top when you inevitably end up there. Make sure you create and maintain close solid relationships in which you can genuinely relax and be yourself.

You are definitely proud, with a sensitive ego. You care about what other people think of you and, despite not appearing to be an obviously emotional person, you can be easily wounded by criticism and slights, either perceived or real. You might not always ask for what you need and deserve, harbouring a secret desire to be seen, heard, acknowledged and recognised for all that you give. Your true nature is bright, bold and vibrant – definitely not a shrinking violet. Always stand up for yourself and follow the path you carve out. Don't allow petty or jealous types into your vicinity. You don't need to be worshipped (although you wouldn't mind) but you do need people around who want the best for you.

The Sun rules the projection of the self – how we express our nature through the way we live and what we focus our attention on. Your career, creative or study achievements, business successes, relationships, family and material acquisitions are all an extension of yourself. You crave spontaneity and aren't afraid to follow your bliss – and then change paths when you decide to follow another form of your bliss. You could become fickle and get caught up in always searching for the next big thing: work on appreciating what you already have and being content with all that is present in your life. Enjoying your achievements and good fortune doesn't mean you are stagnating. Gratitude multiplies your blessings.

1

✦

SUN
DESTINY

———————————◆———————————

DAY

+

MONTH

+

YEAR

=

1

Suns like to be at the beginning and to come first. It's not necessarily an arrogant thing, but more for the pleasure of achievement and earning that place. When the Sun is your destiny planet, you need to take control of your life and always be moving forwards. You like to do, and be, your best and expect excellence from yourself at all times. This can be a good thing for transforming wishes into reality, but it can backfire on you if you never let yourself unwind. Perfectionism is your biggest pitfall in life. To counteract this tendency, tune in to the Sun's optimism, zest for life and ability to enjoy. Cutting loose, at least some of the time, will prevent stress overload. You can afford to lower your expectations a little.

Sun destinies have visions and dreams galore and you really must find the courage within to follow them. Believe in your abilities and work towards your goals. Ambition is your middle name and successful outcomes are mostly inevitable. Enjoy the journey *and* the sense of achievement. You take a lot of pride in everything you do and it boosts your self-esteem when you allow yourself to feel proud of your wins – because you worked hard and earned them. It's in your nature to never rest on your laurels; because of this you can generate a lot of prosperity for yourself. You are a generous soul, too, and like to take care of your loved ones. As you go through life you learn the importance of solid, loving, trustworthy relationships. Cherish your people.

Being in charge is the way you like to roll, and you have excellent leadership skills. Avoid being overbearing or bullish with your team and don't let imposter syndrome steal your joy. You have earned your place at the table. You might not be the most flexible person, but you definitely want to get along with everyone and it serves you to bend a little here and there. Don't base your sense of self-worth on other people's opinions of you (or what you imagine are their worst opinions). Although you are very self-reliant, don't go it alone all the time. You need balance in your life and connections with others, so avoid isolating yourself in an impenetrable tower of aspiration.

Expressing yourself and having faith in your talents is important for you career-wise. When it comes to your skills, you see the potential in any situation. Suns are great in the academic, teaching and health sectors, as maverick entrepreneurs, and in any role that is managerial or directorial. You have the power to create whatever you want and you can express that skill anywhere. The Sun creates opportunity and gives you that go-getter trait, so you are a brilliant leader. You work best alone or in situations where you play the role of coach, mentor, teacher or head honcho. You are the lead singer in the band, no backing role for you. Make sure you have autonomy and freedom to do your thing. Most importantly, you need to be constantly progressing, or you'll die of boredom.

Sun destinies have visions and dreams galore and you really must find the courage within to follow them.

45

1

✦

SUN RELATIONSHIPS

✦ ———————————————————————— ✦

YOUR DESTINY NUMBER

+

THEIR DESTINY NUMBER

=

1

Generosity is the most important thing here, no matter what form this relationship takes in your life. And I'm not talking about material generosity, as nice as that is. Generosity of spirit is what it's all about with Sun connections. Aim to bring out the best in each other. Encourage the other person to be their best self, by first attempting to be your best self. Use positive reinforcement and reassurance to boost the other person's self-belief and confidence. Be each other's strongest ally and advocate. Allow both people the opportunity to share the spotlight and make sure you give as good as you get.

Ego can get in the way of a smooth connection with Sun relationships, so do keep yours in check and don't allow the other person's to dominate either. Independence is important, so let them run their own show and avoid controlling behaviour, comparison, competitiveness and one-upmanship. This alliance works best when you both focus on what you can give to make it as good as it can be. Always focus on seeing the other through the lens of kindness and acting as a true friend. Forgive easily the small slights, stay in a space of love and celebrate all the goodness present between you. So much fun can be had together and this connection can bring great illumination and enlightenment to you both as individuals.

When it comes to Sun love, shine your light on each other as much and as often as you humanly can. Sun relationships have a teacher–pupil vibe and the two of you will play both roles at different times. This romance can be beautifully loving and greatly heighten overall life happiness for both of you. Self-worth issues will inevitably come up in this partnership, so be there for each other to support and affirm when this arises. Always seek to raise each other higher. Be a source of strength and encouragement. Don't let it become a relationship where one of the two makes it all about them and always has their way. Allow room for both of you to be the star and leader. Give generously of your love and allow yourself to receive it, too.

KINDRED
SUN
ASSOCIATES

These are the special friends of the Sun, connected and aligned with the brilliant energy of this magnificent and colossal star. They embody Sun characteristics and can be called upon to support or enhance your Sun energy, whether or not this is one of your celestial bodies. Use this information and work with the Sun to balance, inspire, heal and make magic happen.

POWER COLOUR

ORANGE

Orange is the colour most commonly associated with the Sun. Think
of how the Sun appears as a great ball of orange fire in the sky, with
its orange light strewn across the skies at dusk and dawn. Gold is also
associated with the Sun and is highly valued, representing wealth, success
and the energy and light of the Sun.

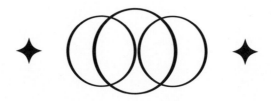

POWER DAY

SUNDAY

Sunday was known as *Sunnandaeg* or 'day of the Sun' by the Anglo-Saxons, *Sondag* by the Norse and *dies Solis* by the Latin-speaking people of ancient times. Sunday is the day for getting back to yourself, putting yourself out there, forging ahead with projects and focusing on plans and dreams.

Boosting vitality is a Sun trait, so anything that supports you having more energy is good to do. Rest is important, especially during busy weeks, as is connecting to your higher self and spiritual practices. Give generously on a Sunday – even if you aren't flush with cash to donate to charities, you can give of your time, energy and love. Add some goodness to life outside yourself in any way you can. The Sun is magnanimous, shining on us all; emulate this quality and show your compassion to the world.

ASTROLOGICAL SIGN	ELEMENT
LEO	**FIRE**

The Sun is known as a fire element planet due to the immense heat, light and energy it radiates from its extraordinarily hot (15 million degrees Celsius) molten core.

TAROT CARDS

The cards of the Magician, Wheel of Fortune and the Sun are numbered 1, 10 and 19 in the major arcana of the tarot deck. The 10 becomes 1 when you add 1 + 0, and 19 becomes 1 when you add 1 + 9 = 10 and then add 1 + 0. When you are practising with or learning the tarot, be aware that these cards represent the energy of the Sun and have Sun-like themes, such as self-advancement, happiness, self-esteem, creating and embracing positive change, spiritual work, the ego and stepping up.

53

BODY NURTURE ZONES

The Sun governs our overall vitality and, more specifically, the eyes, heart and circulatory system. When you have the Sun as one of your planets, make sure you nurture your cardiac system and circulation by staying active and avoiding artery-clogging processed foods. Keep your vitamin D levels up by getting enough sun during safe times of the day – this will help your immune system.

✦————————————————✦

ESSENTIAL OILS

Chamomile

Orange (sweet and bitter)

Petitgrain

Neroli

Rosemary

Sun aromatics have an uplifting vibe. Some are stimulating and refreshing; others are calming mood boosters. You can inhale these oils for their feel-good properties, or dilute and use for massage (avoid the Sun for twelve hours after applying citrus oils).

CHAMOMILE is a common remedy for stress. The oil is used to dispel tension and help you stay calm, like a good, Sun-like friend.

The ORANGES, PETITGRAIN and NEROLI aromatics are closely related. Petitgrain comes from the leaves and neroli from the blossom of the bitter orange tree. The orange tree thrives in warm climates and produces fruit that looks like the Sun. Its oils uplift and increase feelings of happiness.

ROSEMARY is the most stimulating Sun aromatic. A great vitality enhancer, it is considered beneficial for the heart and circulation, both of which are governed by the Sun.

HEALING HERBS

Calendula

Chamomile

Cinnamon

Saffron

Turmeric

The Sun-ruled herbs all have an innate vibrancy, and many also have that gorgeous, happy, orange Sun colour. Some are warming and beneficial as cardiac tonics and for supporting circulation, while others are beautiful lifters that brighten your mood.

CALENDULA and CHAMOMILE are both wonderful anti-inflammatories (especially for hot inflammations) with spirit-lifting, heart-soothing qualities.

CINNAMON is a warming and reviving tonic with aromatic and digestive qualities.

SAFFRON is a traditional mood booster that also offers support to the cardiovascular system.

TURMERIC is now well known as an antioxidant that beautifully assists the cardiovascular system to stay healthy.

MAKE SOME SUN MAGIC

Have a sunbath and infuse yourself with Sun energy (during a safe time of day).

Put on your gold jewellery and vibe magnificent.

Dare to put yourself out there and show the world your talents.

Wear orange, light an orange candle or place a beautiful orange object in your home.

NEEDING INSPIRATION?

Make Sunday your sacred day and do all the things you enjoy.

Celebrate you. Make a list of your best qualities and be proud of who you are.

Keep a gratitude list or journal and write down three things a day you are happy for.

Celebrate solar eclipses and summer solstice each year to welcome more Sun energy and renewal into your life.

FEELING UNBALANCED?

Take time to refocus on activities that make you feel good, rather than those that bring out your inner perfectionist.

Laugh. Boost those happy brain chemicals: hang out with people who give you the giggles, or go and see something funny.

Get involved in community service. The Sun loves to give generously to other people.

SUN
MEDITATION

FOR INCREASING VITALITY

You can do this simple meditation either inside or outside, facing the Sun, if you like. Don't worry if it's a gloomy, cloudy day: the Sun is always there during daylight hours, even if we can't see it. This meditation is extra magical when done around sunrise.

Sit comfortably with a straight posture and
close your eyes if that feels okay for you.

Place your hands, palms up, on your knees in a relaxed way, and
bring the tips of your thumbs to the tips of your ring fingers to
enhance your vital force (in yogic traditions, the ring fingers
connect to the Sun and to the heart).

Imagine the Sun is sitting at heart level in the centre of your chest
and is radiating its enlivening and invigorating energy and light all
through you, bringing its powerful warm glow to every cell of your
body. Focus on the Sun energy and feel it moving through you and
emanating from you as if you were the Sun itself.

Inhale and exhale deeply, gently and slowly for a few minutes
(you can set a timer if this helps).

Take one last deep breath and gently open
your eyes. Now you can go about the rest of
your day with extra Sun power to back you up.

LUMINOUS ◆ INTUITIVE ◆ NURTURING

THE NUMBER 2

✦✦✦

The number 2 represents evolving beyond seeing ourselves as the centre of the universe and beginning to react to and connect, interact, create, intertwine, love and commune with others. It represents the partnerships and relationships between two individuals or entities; in particular, deep family dynamics, marriages and creative collaborations.

Balance – specifically, finding the right balance between two opposing forces, such as the work/life conundrum or differing desires – is highlighted by the number 2. Choices and decisions are a major learning and, to bring out the best of this energy, we need to cultivate adaptability, enhance mutability and reduce resistance so that we don't become stagnant, immovable and old before our time. Wherever there are two sides, people, objects and so on, there is the space between them. This liminal yet dynamic space is where creation and change happens, and 2 helps us to celebrate and cherish this.

Duality, which is often represented metaphorically as two pillars, is the reality of this number. The greatest wisdom 2 offers us is to accept the polarities and instabilities of life, resist any forms of extremism or dogmatism, and learn to be comfortable with the ambiguities and opposing forces expressing themselves all around us. Through this, we can find our own middle path and be ultimately less conflicted.

THE MOON

✦✦✦

While the Sun is 'me', the Moon is 'we'. Ever present in the night sky, the Moon is our constant companion on Earth and changes with time just as we do. The Moon brings light in the darkness of night and has the capacity to dispel negativity and illuminate the unseen. The continuous cycles of birth, death and rebirth are made visible in the darkness as the Moon waxes and wanes above us. The Moon teaches us that nothing is static, change is continual and if we attune ourselves to these rhythms instead of railing against them, life is much easier for us.

The Moon is a satellite of Earth, and the dance between the two is one of constant motion. This hints at the themes of interdependence, co-creation, push and pull, reaction and influence that come with the Moon's energies and directly represent the full spectrum of our relationships with others. The Moon, as the only constant, governs change – the cycles of life, ebb and flow, water and tides, growth, biodynamics, gravity and the digestive process. Diplomacy, loving others, kindness, fertility, the feminine, mothers, children and parenthood and yin principles of softness and receptivity are also the Moon's domain. The Moon's energies are linked to the mystical – dreams, the invisible made visible, the gateway between this world and the unseen world, mystery, creativity and subtle energy.

The Moon has two cycles: the waxing cycle between the new and full Moon, and the waning cycle between the full and new Moon. These represent the dual fundamentals of life: nothing stays the same; you can't continuously expend energy unless you recuperate by resting; there is day and there is night, bright weather and gloomy weather; there are happy feelings and sad feelings. And so, the Moon teaches us about balance, embracing change and unifying opposing forces.

2

✦

MOON FOUNDATION

*DAY
OF THE
WEEK*
**YOU
WERE
BORN**

=

MONDAY

2

M☾N

FOUNDATION · DAY OF THE WEEK YOU WERE BORN = MONDAY

The Moon foundation person is instinctively creative and has the ability to bring that into any situation, from making inspired art to elevating the mundane. You are naturally in tune with the cycles of life and everything in your surroundings. Moon people possess psychic abilities that are easily tapped, and your dreams are very powerful. Moons have a growth mindset and are interested in regeneration, evolution and cultivating the best in any situation.

Those governed by the number 2 and the Moon are gentle, artistic, loving, imaginative, accepting, peaceful, receptive, intuitive, compassionate, empathetic and insightful. You make the ideal confidante and friend, with your calming, nurturing and faithful nature, and wisdom to share. A Moon will sacrifice all they have for the sake of others and treat their relationships as sacred. You are a gift that keeps on giving, always looking for ways to make everything better.

Moon foundations are warm, giving and cooperative, with high levels of empathy (sometimes too high) and emotional intelligence. A Moon's intuitive gifts are substantial and provide the ability to feel into others' energies and emotions. Being able to decode people is a highly useful skill, provided you stay stable within yourself and don't allow yourself to be too affected by external influences. Although you are mutable and go with the flow, you are still centred within the truth of who you are.

Your sensitivity is your superpower. You have the most beautiful ability to be in harmony with the world around you as you feel your way through it. You seek to light the way for yourself and the lucky people who bask in your glow. Moons do tend to be emotional, so it's good to work on your neutrality. A Moon person is not to be underestimated: there is a strong streak of determination beneath that softly serene exterior. Being creative and fertile, Moons have the ability to create lush gardens from even the most barren soil.

Moons often have difficulty following through. Procrastination, indecision and leaving things until the last

66

minute are major pitfalls. Ensure you protect yourself from harsh people, but do also watch out for being overly sensitive. It will only cause you unnecessary stress, while those who upset you carry on, blissfully unaware of your hurt feelings. Find healthy ways to release and control your emotions so that they don't become excessive, control you and deplete your vitality. Cultivate non-reactivity.

Dependency in relationships can be a big problem. You can easily overly identify and enmesh yourself with other people. Your boundaries can be weak, and this can create trouble and toxic resentment for you. You might find yourself over-giving and then developing a martyr complex. Not speaking your truth and standing up for yourself can be an issue and can lead to dishonesty or apathy, neither of which are healthy.

Anxiety is a Moon tendency: you often worry about worst-case scenarios, especially those involving people you care about. Your sensitivity can lead to bewilderment at times, when you don't understand why other people don't feel or care as deeply as you do. Just like the Moon itself, your energy fluctuates, and it is best to accept this and work it into your life rather than forcing yourself to go against the grain. Let yourself wax and wane and learn to live in effortless flow with your own rhythms.

To bring out your best aspects, spend time with your nearest and dearest and cocoon yourself at home whenever you need to rejuvenate. Make your home base your sanctuary and sacred space. Meditation or meditative activities keep you steady and keeping a journal can be useful. Follow your intuition and always listen to it. Balance the giving and taking in your life and make time for yourself. Relationships are, of course, important but put them in their rightful place and maintain your independence. Acknowledge your true feelings and allow them to exist without being too hard on yourself about being a sensitive soul. Boundaries, boundaries, boundaries. And more boundaries. Build them, strengthen them, enforce them.

2

✦

MOON PERSONALITY

DAY
OF THE
MONTH
YOU
WERE
BORN
=
2

Moon personality people are the connectors, carers, empaths and big-hearted lovers of the world. You can create at will, so use that talent wisely. People adore you and are drawn to your loving nature and poetic vibe. You offer comfort and sweetness to those in your circle. Something that is powerful, and often overlooked by Moons, is your ability to enchant people and creatures like magic. You are magnetic, and subtly so. It's as if you have a secret glamour that doesn't need to announce itself; it just emanates gracefully from your person and quietly captivates all within its reach.

The Moon approach to life is all about feeling, and you are instinctively attuned to the world around you. Being able to relate to the full spectrum of life, from animals to nature to people, is another gift. Others gravitate towards you, and you are an absolute natural with people from all walks of life – you can relate to anyone and have a genius level of understanding. Because of this skill, it is important to work on knowing your own mind, forming your own opinions and defending your own truth, so you aren't swept away by the currents of other people's energies.

Because Moons care so deeply about anything and everything, it is not uncommon for your feelings and needs to go unnoticed and unacknowledged. This can wound you a great deal, and if it happens too often you can become closed off and aloof to try to protect yourself from harm. You might also be guilty of suppressing your truth and failing to recognise your own needs – this can create drama in your mind, as you argue with yourself rather than manage the imbalanced situation.

Moons are typically philosophical in their outlook and are naturally very connected to nature, water and the cycles of life. You understand duality and are diplomatic and able to see both sides of the story. A Moon is never the loudmouth in the room, but when you do speak it's usually meaningful and wise, rather than simply idle chatter to fill an empty space.

Moons are not confrontational: you're generally a little bit shyer and more reserved. If there is conflict, you're more likely to be a touch dishonest to keep the peace. Moons will often do what needs to be done to get along with everyone, rather than ruffle feathers. Your intentions are usually good; however, you can be emotionally manipulative when not in balance. This can come out if you feel you're being undervalued in family or relationship dynamics. Because Moons don't necessarily speak up enough, this can lead to resistance, resentment and passive aggressive behaviour.

Moons can be too kind – you won't necessarily tell it straight because you hate to hurt someone's feelings. If a Moon is in a relationship with someone who takes advantage of their sweet nature, it can be difficult to get out because Moons worry about letting others down. You can get caught up and waste time with less scrupulous types because you believe everyone deserves second, third, fourth, fifth and more chances. Don't be a doormat! Don't let people walk over you, mess you about or take you for granted. People might confuse your kindness for being a 'pushover', so be discerning and share yourself only with those who are proven to be worthy. You are more valuable than you realise.

2

✦

MOON
DESTINY

✦————————————————————✦

DAY

+

MONTH

+

YEAR

=

2

Moon people are the gentle folk of the world. Having the Moon as your destiny brings out the nurturer in you and, as you go through life, you are likely to care for a lot of people, plants and animals. Your skill in creating a nourishing community and family everywhere you go is second to none. Your people skills are exceptional and, as you grow older and wiser, your intuition and sensitivity grow, too. You become even better at reading and pre-empting people. Nurturing others by providing the space for them to be who they are is a blessing to the world.

You are very family oriented (whether that family is chosen or inherited) and love to take care of everyone in your brood. You have an innate understanding of the cycles of life and are naturally attuned to the cosmos; particular power comes to you through observing the Moon's phases. Keep honing your intuition; allow your magical self to come through by listening to your inner guidance.

Moons are people people. You love to look after people, be with people, and connect, commune and experience life with people. Being alone is not your thing, but you do need time to recharge because you give a lot of yourself. The Moon is the classic mother archetype – and you're out to parent the world. Someone who has a Moon on side has a guardian for life, which is a great comfort for anyone who is struggling. Moons make great confidantes – you are brilliant at counselling and guiding others towards knowing their own truth. Moon people never impose their thoughts or beliefs on others.

Some examples of the vocations you can excel at are teaching, human resources, people management, sociology, social work, psychology, counselling, childcare, healing, health and wellness work, marketing, PR, horticulture, botany, diplomatic positions, campaigning for good causes and anything creative, especially in regard to the tactile arts. You are genuine, empathetic and have the human touch. This works well in any area dealing with people, behaviours and trend patterns.

2

◆

MOON
RELATIONSHIPS

◆————————————————◆

*YOUR
DESTINY
NUMBER*

+

**THEIR
DESTINY
NUMBER**

=

2

This alliance is all about finding middle ground. There's no room here for stubbornness, selfishness or big egos. The give and take must be evenly distributed, or else. Accept the differences and attune yourself to the ways you complement each other. Stay calm and seek balance. If you are over-giving, learn to keep some energy, love and care for yourself. If you are taking too much, learn to hold yourself up and give yourself what you need without over-burdening the other. The last thing this dynamic needs is the martyr rearing its manipulative head and, in a Moon-ruled relationship, this trap is easy to fall into. If it does come up, deal with it and move on gracefully.

Speaking of being ruled by the Moon, this relationship is constantly evolving and will go through huge phases of growth coupled with times of letting go. Because the Moon's disposition is so centred around relationships, it is important that you also maintain a thriving relationship with yourselves. There is a strong intuitive connection and you can often pick up on the other person's vibe, feel their emotions and know them on an almost telepathic level (however, do watch out for projecting what isn't there and, if in doubt, check in and ask). This is the type of connection where you can finish each other's sentences and sense the person before they walk into a room.

Specifically with love relationships, remember that the Moon waxes and wanes and, similarly, this relationship does not lend itself to stagnation. This love relationship unfolds – it won't be pushed, coerced or forced. Everything changes constantly; don't suffocate the love out of fear or suck it dry from emotional excess. Nurture and care for each other. The pair of you can be beautifully creative together. In this relationship you should be able to be comfortable, reveal your true selves and grow. Going with the flow sounds like a cool way to be but is, in fact, very difficult to master. Surrender the need to control and to know it all. Being each other's guiding lights, providing emotional sustenance and understanding the other on a deep level is truly Moon.

KINDRED
MOON
ASSOCIATES

These are the special friends and correspondences of the Moon, connected to and aligned with the entrancing energy of this magical celestial body. They embody Moon characteristics and can be called upon to support or enhance your Moon energy, whether or not this is one of your planets. Use this information and work with the Moon to balance, inspire, heal and make magic happen.

SILVER AND WHITE

Silver and white are the colours of the Moon
as we see it in the sky. Green also represents the fertility and abundance
of the Moon's influence: plants grow by the cycles of the Moon, and the
Moon itself appears to grow in the sky as it waxes.

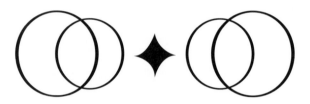

MONDAY

Monday is ruled by the Moon. The Anglo-Saxons gave it the name *Mondandaeg,* meaning 'day of the Moon', from the Norse personification of the Moon, Mani. For anyone with the Moon as one of their numerology planets, every Monday is special and supportive.

Connect with these properties to have a more aligned day. Use your intuition and creative genius on Mondays: we all have this quality. Whether you are tied to a desk in an uninspiring day job, or living your dream, you can be creative in your approach, thinking and expression. Nurturing is a Moon gift, and family, either chosen or inherited, is also in the Moon's sphere of influence. Take some time to connect with and show some love to the most important people, plants and animals in your life. And be sure to nurture yourself as much as you do others, so you remain in balance.

ASTROLOGICAL SIGN

CANCER

ELEMENT

WATER

The Moon influences the tides, all bodies of water on Earth, and all water that contains life forms – as, of course, wherever there is water, there is life.

TAROT CARDS

The cards of the High Priestess, Justice and Judgement are numbered 2, 11 and 20 in the major arcana of the tarot. These all become 2 as single-digit numbers (11 becomes 2 when you add 1 + 1; 20 becomes 2 when you add 2 + 0). When studying the tarot or doing readings, be aware that these cards are associated with the energy of number 2 and the Moon. The classic themes of duality, intuition, magic, mystery and finding the middle way are part of the same wisdom found in these particular cards.

BODY NURTURE ZONES

The Moon governs our reproductive system, urinary system (waters of the body) and digestive system. When the Moon is one of your planets, it is important to nurture and take care of these parts of the body. Staying hydrated and well nourished is imperative.

✦ ─────────────────────────── ✦

ESSENTIAL OILS

Jasmine

Tuberose

Lavender

Clary sage

Spearmint

Moon-ruled aromatic medicines are mostly sedating, floral and hypnotic. These essential oils can be used as inhalants in diffusers or burners for their mood-altering properties, or diluted and applied topically to soothe digestion and ease cramping.

JASMINE and TUBEROSE are both famously more fragrant at night, as is LAVENDER with its silvery foliage. They are all best picked at night for optimum aromatic intensity. All three are sedating and calming – helpful for soothing intense emotions.

CLARY SAGE is a fantastic sedative that also acts as a gentle tonic, helping to restore a burnt-out nervous system. It is also a wonderful dream enhancer.

SPEARMINT is cooling, uplifting, gently refreshing and excellent for easing digestive complaints, without overstimulating a sensitive Moon. It's the perfect pick-me-up for flat moods or to help overcome procrastination.

HEALING HERBS

Corn silk

Hibiscus

Lavender

Spearmint

Marshmallow

On a physical level, Moon herbal allies are cooling, soothing and moistening. They work on balancing, nurturing and assisting the body areas governed by the Moon, which include the reproductive, digestive and urinary systems. All the waters and fluids of the body are covered by the Moon, especially in relation to diuretics, which remove excess water via the kidneys, bladder and urinary tract. On an emotional and psychological level, some Moon herbs temper our emotions, calm mental stress and assist with sleep.

CORN SILK and HIBISCUS are useful as gently diuretic cleansing herbs that might help reduce water retention.

LAVENDER calms frazzled nerves, eases pain and soothes emotions. Many also enlist it to help with sleep.

SPEARMINT is a refreshing yet gentle aid to digestion, while MARSHMALLOW is soothing for an irritated digestive system. Both have a cooling effect.

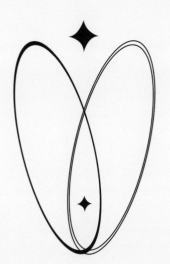

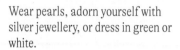

MAKE SOME MOON MAGIC

Wear pearls, adorn yourself with silver jewellery, or dress in green or white.

Be out in the moonlight or under the Moon's gaze.

Celebrate the new and full Moon – eclipses are extra powerful.

Cultivate your intuition by reading tarot or oracle cards.

FEELING UNBALANCED?

Honour your energy levels and practise exemplary sleep hygiene. Take warm baths, nap and get cosy at home.

Create something artistic or make an altar.

Bathe or swim in the ocean, lakes, rivers or pools.

Nurture yourself with wholesome food and drink nourishing herbal teas.

NEEDING INSPIRATION?

Follow the Moon phases and be aware of the energies of the different stages of these cycles. The new Moon is the refresh and renew point; the full Moon is the fruition and completion point. The waxing phase is more outgoing and active, while the waning phase is quiet and inward-looking.

Keep a dream diary and tune in to the messages found in them.

Cultivate some plants or plant a beautiful garden.

Enjoy something creative, something nourishing and something nurturing every Monday.

MOON MEDITATIONS

These simple meditation rituals can be used by anyone, whenever there is a new or full Moon. Use them to honour the significant turning points in the Moon cycle and to bring yourself into alignment with the energies of the waxing and waning phases as they unfold. When you work with the Moon like this, you are moving with the tide instead of swimming against it. These meditations create awareness of when it is a good time to push and when it is smarter to soften. Performing these at night is extra powerful; more so if you can be outside in the moonlight to soak up those magical Moon vibes.

ON THE
✦ NEW MOON ✦

Firstly, light a white candle.

Sit comfortably in a quiet place. Choose and contemplate two specific wishes. Think of happenings you would like to create or scenarios you would like to take action on during the waxing Moon period.

Think of this as the ideal moment to plant the seeds of what you would like to harvest in your life. The waxing moon is a time of setting intentions, renewal, reaching out, new growth, expansion and magnifying your blessings.

See them happening in your mind's eye. Watch as these events unfold and focus on the details as much as you can. Imagine how it will feel to experience them. Consciously choose to trust in your abilities and worthiness.

Write the two wishes on a piece of paper (preferably in silver pen or pencil) and place them in an envelope or jar dedicated to your Moon goals. (Reading them at the dawn of a new year is a beautiful way to contemplate what has been achieved in the year just gone.)

Blow out your candle.

ON THE
✦ FULL MOON ✦

Firstly, light a white candle.

Sit comfortably in a quiet place and contemplate two things you would like to let go of or have gently removed from your life during the waning phase of the Moon cycle. These might be habits you wish to break, or a painful memory or feeling from which you would like to be free.

The waning Moon is the time to let go of situations, thoughts, relationships or emotions that do not serve you in life. It is a time of cleansing and releasing, reducing and paring things back to the all-important essentials. A time to come to the truth of matters and go within.

See yourself free of the things you would like to do without. Feel the lightness that comes with removing heavy burdens or tiresome ways of being. Consciously send them away from you, with love and gratitude for the lessons they have brought you.

Write them on a piece of paper (preferably in silver pen or pencil) and either burn them in the flame of your candle, if you can safely do so, or rip them up and throw them away.

Blow out your candle.

89

JUP
IT
ER

OPTIMIST ✦ **ADVENTURER** ✦ *MAGNIFIER*

THE NUMBER 3

✦✦✦

The number 3 signifies a movement beyond the dual aspects of 2 into something greater; expansion and addition are what 3 is all about. This relates to many aspects of life and our philosophies: the Holy Trinity; the Triple Goddess of Paganism; the 'mind, body and spirit'; and the endless life cycle of birth, death and rebirth. There is also the 'beginning, middle and end' and 'past, present and future', and the three realms of heaven, earth and hell.

Much significance can be attributed to 3. One of the most well-known metaphysical beliefs about 3 is the law of threefold return or 'rule of three' – something many Pagans, Wiccans and mystics swear by. The law states that anything we send out into the universe comes back to us threefold. This is a version of the reciprocity or karmic or 'cause and effect' belief that returns the energy of a sender's actions to them, multiplied. For better or worse, our every thought, word and deed create an effect in the universe that will catch up with us eventually; 3 is considered to be the magnifying force.

Luck is also associated with 3. Who hasn't heard that 'bad luck comes in threes' or 'the third time's the charm'? Apparently, in our earliest times, we had a word for the number 2 but no word for 3, just a word for 'many'; perhaps this is why 3 has always been associated with increase. The number 3 is represented symbolically as a triangle; the mystical meanings of the triangle include balance, ascension, magic, wisdom, the manifestation of desires and the path to divinity. The Three Fates of Greek mythology were three sister goddesses of destiny; they had power over when every life began, the length and destiny of each life, and when it was fated to end. The number 3 asks us to strike a delicate balance between controlling our own fate and surrendering to it.

JUPITER

✦✦✦

Jupiter is named for the king of the Roman gods, who was associated with the skies, lightning and thunder, charity, luck and royalty. This god was known for bestowing riches, abundant harvests, blessings and favours on those who worshipped him, and the planet is known as the planet of largesse. It is credited with material beneficence, wealth, abundance, excess, generosity and charitable giving. Jupiter expresses the dynamic energy of growth, optimism, good times and good luck.

Jupiter magnifies, exaggerates, boosts and expands. Whatever this planet touches becomes larger and greater than it was before. A lot of people go straight to the money and finance factor when they consider Jupiter's influence, but it also governs other kinds of high-value inner riches that money cannot buy. Jupiter is the ruler of the gods and of 3; therefore, ascension and spiritual wealth are major parts of this planet's power.

Jupiter is the largest planet in our solar system (over twice the size of all the other planets combined). It has no discernible solid surface, endures extreme temperatures and has a massively strong magnetic field. This huge planet has, at last count, seventy-nine moons, four sets of rings and an ocean of liquid hydrogen that is the largest of all the oceans in the solar system. Jupiter takes around twelve years to complete one rotation of the Sun. The planet is covered in clouds and storms, with one storm of crimson clouds – the Great Red Spot – that is larger than Earth and has raged for centuries. So, Jupiter is by no means a wallflower of a planet.

3

✦

JUP
IT
ER

93

3

✦

JUPITER FOUNDATION

✦————————————✦

DAY
OF THE
WEEK
**YOU
WERE
BORN**

=

THURSDAY

3

JUP IT ER

Jupiter has a dazzling energy and is a never-ending source of positivity. This foundation placement gives you an innate optimism, loads of talent, plenty of intensity and the uncanny ability to make everything turn out great, no matter how dire it appears to be. Jupiters bring hope to the most hopeless of situations. You are able to lift up a scene just by walking into it. The Thursday-born Jupiter is a force of nature, full to the brim and overflowing with enthusiasm, passion, lustre and talent. You truly can be anything you want – within the reasonable laws of nature – although, even then, miracles are firmly housed within Jupiter's domain.

Nothing can stop you. There is nothing you can't overcome and nothing that can't be improved by your presence. Jupiter foundations may not realise this, but they are the wave that lifts others up and brings huge amounts of wonder, delight and happiness to other people's lives. Jupiter people can carry big ideas through to fruition. You can also carry big concepts, big thoughts and big feelings as if they weighed as much as a feather. You are the person others come to for encouragement, and to help turn dreams into reality. If something can be manifested, trust a Jupiter to make it happen.

Jupiters can be so bright that they attract jealousy. There is a royal, shiny, larger-than-life vibe to Jupiter people that some others just can't handle. Too bad for them. Jupiter foundations do not shrink; you always increase, go further, become more. 'I grow to be great' is the perfect Jupiterian mantra. Never one to rest on your laurels, you will always seek to be the absolute best you can be. Likewise, you will also seek to bring out the best in even the worst situation.

Your Jupiterian optimism can appear to some as ignorance of the harsh realities of the world, but they are just being negative. The truth is, you know how hard life can be, you simply choose to focus on the wonderful parts of being alive and refuse to get bogged down in misery. Everyone needs a Jupiter friend around to pull them out of the mud and remind them of the good things in life. A Jupiter definitely won't commiserate for long about whatever difficulties someone is facing, preferring instead to get that person 'up and at 'em' again. Anyone looking for an extended period of empathy should seek out a Moon or Venus, but if someone needs to reclaim their lust for life, the Jupiter foundation is their go-to.

Sometimes, the desire to avoid difficult feelings or hardships is highly pronounced in the Jupiter foundation, and you might go to great lengths to avoid these things. You will often be unavailable to anything or anyone you don't want to deal with, preferring to go where the living is easy. You can find it difficult to deal with anything negative. This might show up in the form of excess, especially problematic food intake (eating your feelings?), and over-consumption of alcohol or mind-altering substances. Watch out for this tendency, and seek to moderate your intake so this is kept in balance.

Jupiter people value freedom and independence, and you don't like to be boxed in, tied down or restricted. Travel and adventure are a must: you have a strong desire to take in the whole world, to experience as much as possible and to generally live large. Money usually comes to Jupiters with relative ease, as you're aligned with its energy. You seem to attract it, are able to make lots of it and be connected to it without too much trouble. Your attitude to money is often quite relaxed and you are notoriously generous, so if you're a Jupiter it's important to be respectful of the privileges money can afford you and take good care of your finances.

A Jupiter foundation can have mild delusions of grandeur, be a bit grandiose, dream of the perfect life and feel entitled to have it, and believe they are extra special. (It's true, though: you are!) While you can absolutely create a magnificent lifestyle with plenty of comfort if you apply yourself, it's important not to forget the other aspects of life and give energy to your inner world, too, so that you can thrive in both directions. Jupiters are not hugely interested in dull practicalities or anything resembling the mundane everyday: you are a big-picture person with an incredible ability to envision the grandest of schemes.

3

JUP IT ER

FOUNDATION ● DAY OF THE WEEK YOU WERE BORN = THURSDAY

You are also quite brave, willing to take a chance, try anything once and give things a go that many others would be too chicken to attempt.

To bring out the best in Jupiter, it's important to know when to hold back and when to give yourself freedom to fly. Abundance is your middle name, so work on creating the most benefit from what you have, while learning how to decrease what you don't enjoy in a way that is balanced and grounded (rather than simply avoiding things you don't like). Use your sense of adventure to your advantage and explore as much of the world as you can, in whatever way you can. A job involving travel is a great way to make that happen. Hold on to your hope at all times; it's your gift to others and a much-needed commodity in the world. Maintain your health and wellbeing by reining in excessive tendencies (remember, too little can be just as harmful as too much). Also remember that you magnify everything, so focus on what you want to increase.

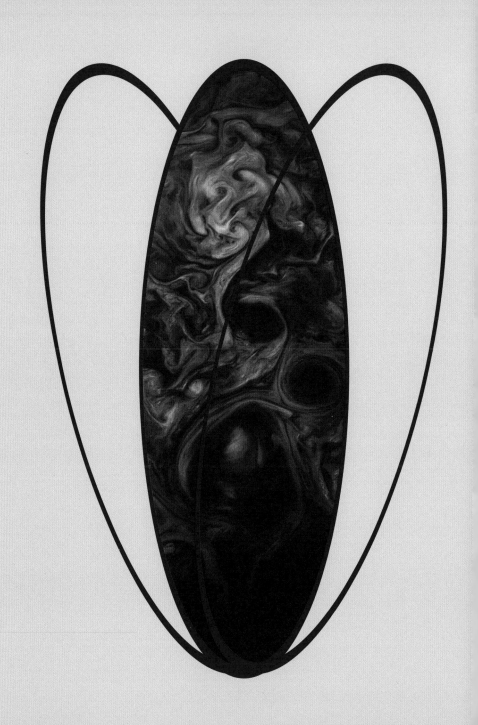

3

✦

JUPITER PERSONALITY

✦ ———————————————— ✦

DAY
OF THE
MONTH
YOU
WERE
BORN

=

3

The Jupiter personality is definitely extroverted in the way they express themselves in the world. People with Jupiter in this placement have a big, bright, powerful energy – unapologetically yourself, you take up space without hesitation. Although perfectly happy in your own company, you excel at bringing out the best in other people, and they love you for it. Jupiters are true team players and you want everything you're involved in to be as good as possible. You won't grab all the credit, though: your nature is more altruistic and you love to be part of things more than you love being seen as the head honcho.

This personality type is naturally happy-go-lucky and fun. You look on the bright side of life and towards the future, with all its brilliant possibilities and wondrous potentials. Jupiters love to laugh – at life, at themselves and at everything else. Your vibe is buoyant and you leave the serious stuff where it belongs, for serious situations only. Strong of character and full of powerful magic, the Jupiter personality can create pretty much whatever they put their considerable energy behind. You're easily bored, though, so that project had better be – and stay – interesting, or you'll be on to the next thing. When you focus your will and put in the work, you can bring into being whatever you choose to make happen.

When Jupiters direct their energy, it is like waving a wand. Energy flows in your chosen direction as if drawn by a magnetic force. Your dreams are grand – if anyone can bring them to life, it's a focused Jupiter. This talent is very useful for any business or creative enterprise. For those with this personality placement, it's important to keep an eye on the prize, maintain a big-picture vision and not get too weighed down by minutiae: that's what other people are there for. Hand that stuff over to them and focus on your ideal outcome. Outsource anything boring that you can afford to outsource, so you can stay in the flow state of growing your lush garden.

Although Jupiters are a lot of fun to be around, and many mistake your childlike ability to be happy in the moment as naivety, you are spiritually very deep and have a natural connection to the higher realms. It doesn't matter what you call it, but you do have a direct line to the divine and a strong bond with the holy and sacred comes easily to you. You do extra well when you cultivate spiritual, as well as material, wealth. Jupiters prefer to live lightly, and carrying heavy emotional baggage doesn't resonate with you. You have a move-on mentality – rather than ruminating and raking over the coals, it's better for you to keep moving towards your dream scenario.

Jupiter is the planet of benevolence and the Jupiterian personality loves philanthropy. Even if you aren't exactly heaving with coin, you love to share your blessings, give to others in need and support worthy causes. Contributing to making the world a better place, in any way that is possible, brings Jupiter a lot of satisfaction. This charitable inclination provides you with a strong social conscience, and you can't stand inequality (although Jupiters do like to be rich, they also want to give of their wealth). Jupiters can be a bit foolhardy, so definitely avoid gambling and taking big risks, as sometimes you will be a little too sure of yourself.

Don't get into the binge–purge cycle of indulgence followed by punishment and extreme restriction. Excess is the Achilles heel of the Jupiter personality – this can manifest in excess of restriction and withholding, as much as it can overindulgence and insatiability. Jupiter personalities also don't like to become enmeshed with other people or live in anyone else's pocket. Your ideal companions provide plenty of freedom to just be yourself without feeling confined in a certain role. A love of your own company, and the love of doing your own thing, is behind that. A Jupiter's wings simply cannot be clipped.

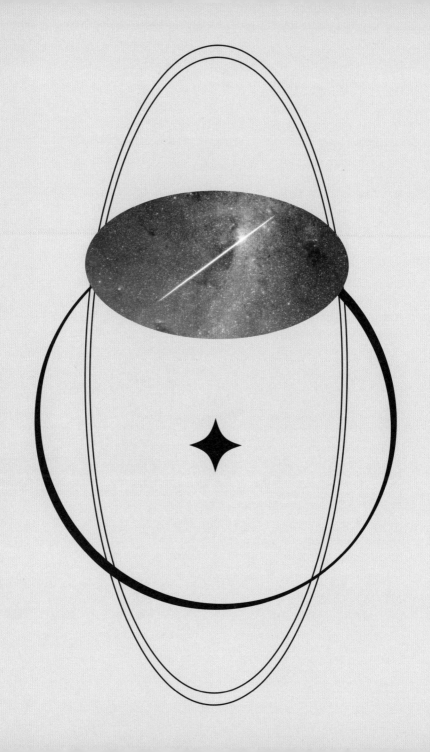

3

✦

JUPITER DESTINY

✦━━━━━━━━━━━━━━━━✦

DAY

+

MONTH

+

YEAR

=

3

The destiny placement of Jupiter gives you the Midas touch. Everything you touch can truly turn to gold if you believe in your abilities, do the foundation work and maintain your vision. As Jupiter is known as the greater benefic (good-doer), whatever you want to create for yourself must also provide benefit for the greater good. By attaching altruistic motives to your desires, you will have supportive energy behind you and can bring those fantastic schemes into reality. Your visionary nature is a treasure and you have the capacity to turn the tiniest spark of an idea into a massive inferno of brilliance. 'Go big or go home' is the Jupiter motto. Why bother doing something by half and keeping things low level, when you can take it so much higher?

Confidence and self-belief are key themes of the Jupiter destiny placement. Often people with this placement can be late bloomers – you take a while to accept your skills and talents and find faith in yourself. Obviously, it's not helpful to consider yourself the best of the best and walk around with a massive ego, but acknowledging your blessings, making the most of what you've got and being proud of your achievements is a good thing. A balanced, healthy self-esteem is important for everyone, even more so for Jupiter destinies. Believe in the power of you. Take up space: don't shrink to make others feel comfortable. Let them feel the discomfort and either choose to go big themselves or stay small. Don't let anyone put you down or undermine your achievements. Your gifts belong to you.

Because Jupiter is the planet of excess, sometimes you need to rein it in a little and stay grounded. Make sure the foundations are solid before you build another level.

Ambitious and idealistic, you like to push beyond limitations and go for gold. Whatever you do, you want it to be the best, the greatest, to go the furthest and grow the largest. Sustainable growth is a mindset that is helpful for you, to keep things balanced. You can always elevate and reach for another goal, but timing it so that you don't overreach is better for your wellbeing. There is much to do, experience and be in life, and you want a lot of doing, being and experiencing. Be aware of a tendency to overcommit, which can rob you of the ability to enjoy any of it.

A Jupiter destiny can truly be a Renaissance human, as they are great at most things they turn their hand to. You have the capability to excel in any career you choose. Jupiters don't like fiddly, small work: you are big-picture people. Some areas that are particularly suited to your energy are the performing arts, events, anything to do with wealth and prosperity (make sure you watch that risk-loving streak), the restaurant business (Jupiters love food) and anything to do with growth, from agriculture to business consulting. Jupiters are excellent at making other people's work go far – you make the best agents, team leaders and managers. Anything involving distribution suits, because you like to cover ever larger areas and create increase. Other suitable areas are philanthropy and charity, self-help and spiritual expansion. Jupiters are great at teaching other people how to live well.

3

✦

JUPITER RELATIONSHIPS

✦ ——————————————————— ✦

YOUR
DESTINY
NUMBER
+
THEIR
DESTINY
NUMBER
=
3

3

JUP IT ER

The Jupiter connection is the visionary connection. You are able to boost each other's faith in the possible goodness of every life situation. You believe in each other and always seek to lift each other up; petty jealousy and competitiveness can't touch you. This relationship works best when you truly want the best for each other, and if that's not currently where it's at, this can be changed by giving more encouragement and showering each other with love. Sing each other's praises. Acknowledge and vocalise the brilliance of the other. Interdependence is the ideal here: it's not a good idea to put too many restraints on a Jupiter alliance; the freedom to be is the greatest gift Jupiter gives. Stay in flow by always aiming for the best in yourself, and by aiming to bring out the best in them.

Adventure calls with this connection, and you expand your horizons through knowing each other. Whether this is a friendship, work association, family tie or love relationship, don't get stuck in a rut, but make merry and do fun and interesting things together. Develop visions together and keep exploring, discovering, journeying, learning and growing. A dream shared is a dream magnified and the Jupiter connection is the 'dreams coming to life' connection. You can support each other and be each other's cheer squad. Everyone needs someone to believe in them and in the Jupiter alliance this is an absolute non-negotiable. This combination can make beautiful things happen. Enjoyment is crucial to this relationship, so live it up a little.

An exquisite love relationship of expansion, this romance can take you both further than you thought possible. This is not a 'kick back and let it all hang out' vibe – you have to keep it fresh. The question with this relationship is always: how can we take this beyond and make it better and greater? There are always new avenues of exploration to travel together and there is always more to achieve. In this romance you experience greater closeness through having pet projects and goals to work towards. This is about how you can treat life as something that can be ever moving towards growth, both as individuals and as a couple. You must give each other freedom and find freedom as a couple. Absolutely avoid taking each other for granted: be fair and share the load. This relationship demands equality. It is important that you have a shared vision for your life. You need to have dreams to follow, something to strive for and something to move towards. You grow to be great together.

A dream shared is a dream magnified and the Jupiter connection is the 'dreams coming to life' connection.

KINDRED JUPITER ASSOCIATES

These are the special friends
and correspondents of Jupiter,
connected and aligned with
the entrancing energy of
this massive and expansive
planet. They embody Jupiter
characteristics and can be called
upon to support or enhance your
Jupiterian energy, whether or not
this is one of your planets. Use
this information and work with
Jupiter to balance, inspire, heal
and make magic happen.

INDIGO

Jupiter is associated with deep blue indigo. The Ancient Egyptians were the first to use blue, which they made by crushing lapis lazuli stones. Until modern times, this colour was prohibitively expensive to produce, regardless of the method, so only the rich and the royal were able to obtain it, hence the term 'royal blue'. It is rather fitting for Jupiter's reputation as the planet of luck and riches.

POWER DAY

THURSDAY

Thursday is Thor's day, named after the Norse god of thunder, the sky (like his Roman counterpart, Jupiter), warriors and fertility (Jupiter is the planet of achievement and growth). Expand your horizons on Thursdays. Jupiter loves to explore, and wants us to experience as much as possible and get the most out of life. Always up for adventure, Jupiter has an optimistic and hopeful attitude. Lift your spirits and surround yourself with inspiration.

Thursday is the best day to focus on generating money, either for yourself or on behalf of others. Because Jupiter magnifies everything it touches, make sure your intentions and attention are on what you would like to happen, not on what you don't want. Work on your self-belief and confidence on Thursdays. Back yourself, go for what you really aspire to do and who you really aspire to be.

ASTROLOGICAL SIGN	ELEMENT
# SAGITTARIUS	# SPACE

Ether (also referred to as space) is Jupiter's element. Known as the fifth element, ether is the invisible energy that permeates space and into the heavens. It is the largest of all the elements and the medium through which the vibrations of sound travel.

TAROT CARDS

The cards of the Empress, the Hanged Man and the World are numbered 3, 12 and 21 in the major arcana of the tarot, with 12 becoming 3 when you add 1 + 2, and 21 becoming 3 when you add 2 + 1. When looking at the tarot, be aware that these cards are ruled by 3 and Jupiter. Their themes of higher causes, growth, exploration, success, abundance, living in the moment and personal evolution are all Jupiterian.

115

3

BODY NURTURE ZONES

The liver, digestion of fats and fat metabolism are all governed by Jupiter. Jupiter is a known encourager of overindulgence, which gives the liver a beating and can make us thick around the middle. Assisting digestion and supporting the liver and metabolism are the prime health focus for Jupiters. Everything in moderation.

ESSENTIAL OILS

Clove

Nutmeg

Lemon balm

Frankincense

Hyssop

The Jupiter essential oils are associated with wealth and spiritual expansion or purification. They can be evaporated in diffusers or burners for their mood-enhancing properties, or to help attract money to yourself. A few can be diluted and massaged into the skin to assist digestion.

CLOVE, NUTMEG, LEMON BALM and FRANKINCENSE are all associated with wealth and generous abundance.

HYSSOP and frankincense are both purifying and clearing, which helps Jupiters to maintain an energetic lightness. Frankincense aids spiritual growth and expansion.

Nutmeg, lemon balm and hyssop are all helpful for digestion and stomach aches when diluted and massaged into the abdomen (after a bout of Jupiterian overindulgence).

HEALING HERBS

Dandelion

Schisandra

Nutmeg

Hyssop

Lemon balm

The herbal friends of Jupiter are often warming and moistening. They work on supporting, healing and generally nurturing the Jupiter body systems of digestion and the liver, which go hand in hand. Gently detoxifying any excesses and protecting the liver are Jupiter's health goals. The herbs that help with digestion also help Jupiter to stay energetically light and reduce the airy quality that can cause an uncomfortable stomach.

DANDELION and SCHISANDRA support liver function, helping the body to naturally cleanse and remove unhelpful compounds.

NUTMEG, HYSSOP and LEMON BALM are firm friends of the digestive system and beneficial in reducing digestive discomfort.

Lemon balm helps maintain a sense of calm and is a famous spirit-lifter that keeps the optimism flowing.

JUP IT ER

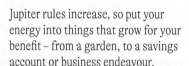

MAKE SOME JUPITERIAN MAGIC

Jupiter rules increase, so put your energy into things that grow for your benefit – from a garden, to a savings account or business endeavour.

Put on a foodie feast for friends. Jupiter loves excess, fine fare and drinks.

Make your work accessible to as wide an audience as possible. Outreach brings blessings to your door.

Wear deep blue hues and bask in the wealth that this colour emanates.

FEELING UNBALANCED?

Go on a random adventure somewhere fresh, for the sheer fun of it.

Go within and take some quiet time as an antidote to the major energy output of goal pursuit.

Meet some new people and let their stories and different expressions of humanity inspire you.

Connect with your chosen source of spiritual nourishment.

NEEDING INSPIRATION?

Make Thursday the day you spend time pouring love into your big dreams and schemes.

Write a list of all the great things in your life to remind yourself of the good stuff, as well as the potential for more.

Do something charitable – giving for the sake of giving is divine.

Inspire yourself. Wear your fabulous individuality loud and proud.

JUPITER MEDITATION

FOR PROSPERITY

✦
|
|
|
✦

This meditation ritual can be performed by anyone wanting to increase their prosperity and draw greater good fortune to themselves. When you wish to create more wealth and opportunities for greater financial expansion, you need your intention, vision, words and actions to align. Jupiter is the lucky planet, but we also need to pave the way for that luck to find us. It's also beneficial when you want to magnify your prosperity to give thanks and give back. This meditation ritual incorporates all these elements to help you with the creation of your bounty.

Light a candle, if you have one handy
(even better if it's a deep blue hue) and sit
or lie down in a comfortable position.

Intention: Choose what you would like to create in the realm of prosperity and how you would like to share a portion of your good fortune with the world.

Vision: Close your eyes for a few minutes and see yourself receiving these gifts, enjoying them and sharing part of them towards a greater good. Don't limit yourself to this through one avenue; stay open to all possibilities and flex your imagination muscle. Wealth can flow in from any direction.

Words: Write your vision on a piece of paper to put in your wallet and say out loud three times. Ask for this to come to you without causing harm and say thank you. Snuff out your candle.

Actions: Now get out there and do the thing (or, even better, three things) that makes it possible for you to reap those blessings.

URANUS

NON-CONFORMIST ❖ **INVENTIVE** ❖ *GENIUS*

THE NUMBER 4

✦✦✦

The number 4 has some interesting connotations and inspires great differences of opinion. Many people associate 4 with structure and conventional personality traits. Some of this definitely rings true when you consider the four cardinal directions, the four corners of the Earth, the four sides of a square and the four visible elements. The number 4 is a representation of matter and that which we can grasp and see. But this is not the whole picture.

There is more to reality than meets the eye and 4 also asks us to consider that which we can't see or grasp within our limited scope. When we relate 4 to structure, we must also understand that structures are there to provide the foundation point for jumping off and exploring other options. Structures can be rebuilt, redefined and re-created. Matter and what eclipses matter are intertwined. Therefore, to re-create, there must first be chaos. Although 4 represents matter, the lessons of 4 lie in how to break through the restraints of our physical selves, free ourselves from unhealthy attachments to the material world and, in so doing, recover our true essence. This is why the number 4 and the planet Uranus are considered to be the disruptors.

Number 4 rules transformation and the principles of alchemy. Do not fear the transformative and reinventive energies of 4. Embracing uncertainty makes us creative collaborators in the process of living. It is a natural part of life to either change or have change thrust upon us (the former is usually preferable). We are *meant* to create, destroy and recreate. That's the juicy bit. Life is a continuous process of birth, life, death and rebirth. There is no evolution without revolution.

URANUS

♦♦♦

Uranus is named for Ouranos, a Greek god of the sky and personification of heaven. This wild maverick is one of the two distant planets in our solar system that aren't visible to the naked eye. Uranus rules the unconventional, unusual and unique; it is the planet of genius, ingenuity, invention and reinvention. Restructuring, reorganising, rebellion and revolution are all firmly in the Uranian domain. Known as a great disruptor, Uranus turns things upside down and inside out. This almost always ends up being for the best, even if it's uncomfortable at the time. Uranus will bring delusions crashing down and has neither the time nor the inclination to mollycoddle anyone's ego.

Uranus rules the number 4 and is geometrically represented by the four sides of the square, which traditionally represents matter. But Uranus is about breaking rules, transcending matter and inventing new ways of doing, being and seeing. Liberation and freedom from the status quo are pure Uranus. Expect the unexpected when this quirkster is around.

The mysteries of Uranus are many, but we have managed to glean morsels of information over the years. Thirteen rings, only visible by mega-telescope, circle the planet and were discovered in 1977, nearly 200 years after the planet was first seen through a telescope. Uranus has a marked tilt to one side, which affects its orbital pattern. It is icy cold, rotates backwards, has strange seasonal timelines (imagine a winter that lasts twenty-one years) and takes eighty-four years to orbit the Sun. Uranus was thought to be a star or a comet until we were able to observe it at higher magnification, so it's a trickster in that way. This kind of ingenuity and non-conformism is a classic Uranian trait.

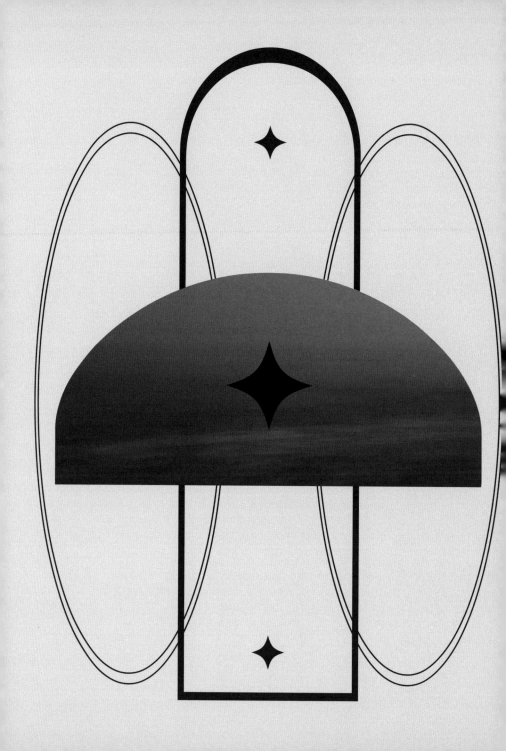

4

✦

URANUS
FOUNDATION

◆━━━━━━━━━━━━━━━━━━━━━━━◆

*URANUS DOES NOT HAVE
A FOUNDATION PLACEMENT,
AS THERE IS NO DAY
OF THE WEEK NAMED
AFTER URANUS*

4

✦

URANUS PERSONALITY

✦————————————————————✦

DAY
OF THE
MONTH
YOU
WERE
BORN

=

4

URANUS

Innovation lies in the gap between how things are and how you want them to be. This is the gift of the Uranian personality placement. Your ingenuity, originality and inventiveness are your magical powers. You are often ahead of the curve in your outlook. Many a Uranus personality grows up lonely and feeling like an outsider. Difficulty fitting in is a big challenge to endure – no one wants to be looked at as if they're from another planet. It is quite common for Uranus personalities to act the conventional role and either have a wild, secret inner or hidden life or, in the worst-case scenario, suppress their uniqueness.

The world seriously needs your brand of brilliance, so don't hide it away. You are unique and uniquely gifted. Uranus bestows upon you the ability to see, feel, think about and experience the world in a different way. Uranus people are the changemakers of the world, creating new ways of doing and sharing new ways of being. You break away from the norm and explore the unconventional, to bring fresh ideas and perspectives into the world. Uranus in this placement makes you an explorer, keen to uncover, discover and understand more. Uranian personalities often have very broad and unconventional interests. You generally don't care what's fashionable or considered 'normal'; you like what you like and that's it.

Uranus people are firing on all cylinders intellectually. Your mind buzzes with thoughts and ideas and you can be analytical and meta, thinking about anything and everything. It is common for Uranus personalities to be genius-level thinkers and have very special skills. This planet gives you the ability to go deep with your thinking and understand at a level beyond many other people. You can be insightful, thoughtful and philosophical and often have profound wisdom within you (although you might not always choose to share it). Sometimes your presence can feel remote – you might be caught up in your mind and whatever you are currently focusing on. Detachment isn't as difficult for a Uranian as it is for others.

Freedom is an absolute essential for the Uranus personality. You cannot be in situations where you are restricted, or feel you're not accepted for who you really are. Find the funny quirksters that you can be quirky with. Most Uranus people are hilarious, with a cheeky sense of humour and a wit that exposes the absurdities of life. Definitely not a follower, you are meant to go your own way. In love relationships, the most important thing is for you to have acceptance, the freedom to be yourself and plenty of space to follow your own interests without being made to feel guilty. An overly needy partner is not for you.

Rebelliousness is in your nature. Even if you appear to play by the rules, you will often have your own special ways of flouting them. So, while you might not be shouting your dissent from the rooftops, you are probably engaging in some quiet rebellion in one way or another. You like to cover your bases and get the basics sorted out and, from there, play with life and enjoy yourself – although this might not come until you are older, as many Uranus personalities bury themselves in work. This workaholism can either be because you are obsessed with and love what you do, or to avoid self-work or awkward personal interactions (and sometimes both).

The concept of alchemy resonates when you have this planet ruling your personality. Your approach to transformation means you are ready to interact with the minor and major shifts that happen constantly within both you and your surroundings. Instead of rallying against them, the best strategy for a Uranian personality is to situate yourself at the centre of them. You are highly suited to creating and leading change. Change really is the only constant in life and the more you accept it, create it, collaborate and roll with it, the happier you will be. You are ever the phoenix rising from the ashes to begin again.

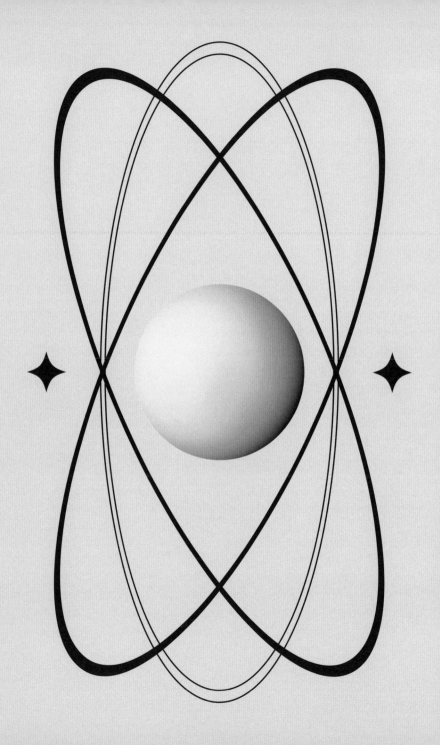

4

✦

URANUS
DESTINY

✦————————————————————✦

DAY

+

MONTH

+

YEAR

=

4

A forward-thinking maverick who loves to be at the forefront of everything, the Uranus destiny has an impressive pioneering spirit. You invigorate those around you with your lively mind, popping out fresh perspectives like there's no tomorrow. This isn't a destiny planet for the faint-hearted. You are meant to be creative, to explore, to think differently, to vibe revolutionary and to come up with new solutions to old problems. With Uranus in this placement, you have a lightning-fast mind and vast intellectual capacity, with less emphasis on emotion. Sometimes you move so quickly that you might struggle to keep up with yourself – you can be the classic eccentric professor type, caught up in your visionary internal world while unaware of, and disengaged from, the mundane.

Speaking of the mundane, it can be a struggle for Uranus destinies to care about the boring matters you are supposed to care about as an adult living on Earth. It's not necessarily easy to fit the status quo either; but, as you go through life and gain more freedom, you can find your group of lovable, quirky individuals to mind-meld with. So, if you're currently feeling like a massive outsider, don't despair: there are plenty of other misfits in the world and some of them are your people. Your unusualness is a blessing, because you offer a wonderfully distinctive point of difference in how you perceive and think. You are the rebel, the rabble-rouser, the iconoclast. This is your talent.

Original and a bit of a character, the Uranian destiny is hugely refreshing to have around. Although you might not be the biggest people person out there (depending on what else you have going on in your planets) you are a delightful eccentric who breaks with convention and opens things up. They say necessity is the mother of invention, and you are able to create brilliant solutions, designs, concoctions and contraptions. Never one to follow, you can do what nobody else has, and achieve what has never been achieved before. You don't shadow the crowd, you initiate. You don't do trends, you do *you*.

Philosophy, tech and science are areas where you excel, for obvious reasons. But you truly have the blessing of being able to explore, create, invent and theorise in a completely new way, no matter what field you end up working in (and many Uranus destinies change careers dramatically at least once in a lifetime). You can take the most traditional, set-in-stone subject and design and devise a whole new version of it. The most important thing for this placement is that you have freedom to spread your wings and aren't penned in. You absolutely suit doing your own thing, running your own business and working solo, too – you will be able to keep yourself interested and motivated if you are challenged enough by the work.

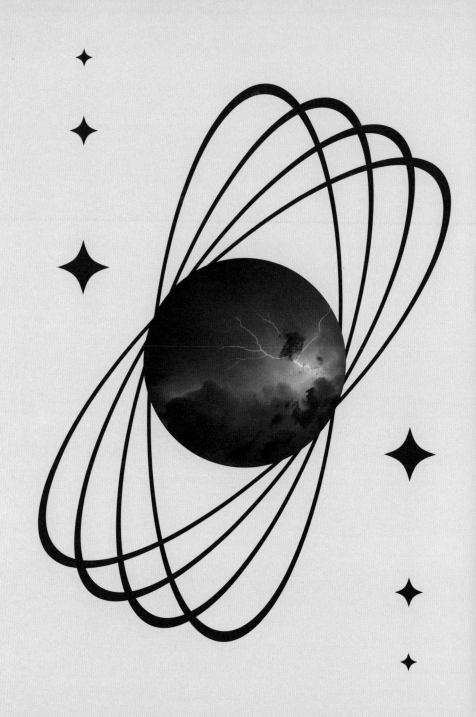

4

✦

URANUS RELATIONSHIPS

✦———————————————✦

YOUR
DESTINY
NUMBER
+
THEIR
DESTINY
NUMBER
=
4

I call this one the 'ego challenge' relationship. This relationship will test you – and the point of that test is to grow. It's all about transformation with Uranus, and transformation is woven into every part of the endless cycle of birth, life, death and rebirth. So, through knowing each other, parts of you will have to be let go and parts of the other person will have to be let go, too. You will also have plenty of opportunities to bring in new ways of thinking, feeling, doing and being. This revolutionary, change-heavy vibe doesn't mean you trick yourself into putting up with harmful shenanigans because it's 'teaching' you. What it means is that this relationship is designed to make you develop as a person.

If you have a 4 connection going on and you're reading this thinking your relationship is easy-breezy and you have no idea what I'm banging on about, perhaps think again. It could be the challenge is to not get too comfy or take anything for granted with this person, unless you fancy a cosmic shock! Uranus will create upheaval and make things very uncomfortable if you get too complacent. The Uranus alliance makes sure you continue to grow and develop yourself. This relationship needs to be in a dynamic, moving state to reach its fullest potential. And the potential is centred around changing each other for the better. Evolution is not always the easiest road, but it is the most worthwhile; although this energy is demanding and intense, you will learn a great deal.

Uranus love matches are not for the faint-hearted. This romance can turn your world on its head. That's not necessarily a bad thing, but it does require a certain fortitude and commitment to pull it off. Unconventional is the perfect word to describe a Uranian pairing. You two can create a fulfilling, sublimely loving and conscious relationship that suits you both. There's no shirking the work, though. That goes for both people. This love will change you, sometimes in subtle yet far-reaching ways, and sometimes in hugely obvious bombshell ways. Are you ready for that? It's okay to walk away if the answer is no. Uranian relationships wake us up if we are falling asleep at the wheel; they are designed to re-create us so that we can shed our tired old skin and renew ourselves. When you choose this relationship, choose it fully and love with your whole heart. Accept that everything that shows up (and much will) is happening so that you both evolve as people. You are each other's awakening.

Uranus love matches are not for the faint-hearted. This romance can turn your world on its head.

KINDRED URANUS ASSOCIATES

These are the special friends of Uranus, connected and aligned with the renewing and metamorphic energy of this wild planet. They embody Uranus characteristics and can be called upon to support or enhance your Uranian energy, whether or not it is one of your planets. Use this information and work with Uranus to balance, inspire, heal and make magic happen.

POWER COLOURS

BLUE AND GREY

Electric blue, which is likened to the colour of lightning and has a fast, dynamic and enlivening vibe to it, is Uranus in colour form. Grey, which represents in-between worlds and liminal space, is also associated with Uranus because of the unseen qualities of the planet. And so is light blue, due to the colour of this planet.

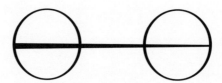

POWER DAY

THERE IS
NO DAY
OF THE WEEK
NAMED
AFTER
URANUS

ASTROLOGICAL SIGN

AQUARIUS

ELEMENT

SPACE

Uranus governs the fifth element, known as space or ether. This realm or quality is unseen, yet hugely influential in our lives. You can't see gravity, but without it you would float off the face of the Earth.

In ancient astrology Aquarius was ruled by Saturn.

TAROT CARDS

The cards of the Emperor and Death are numbered 4 and 13 in the major arcana of the tarot, and 13 becomes 4 when you add 1 + 3. When looking at the tarot it is helpful to know that both these cards carry Uranus energy and have Uranian wisdom to share in bringing breakthroughs, revolution and transformation, bringing order to what is chaotic, staying true to yourself, avoiding recklessness, aiding transformation, and weeding out the old so that the new can sprout.

BODY NURTURE ZONES

Looking after your nervous system, brain chemistry and mental health is extra important when Uranus is one of your planets. Because Uranus is intense, fast and attuned to etheric energy, you are likely to be sensitive, so it is helpful to stay grounded and remove unnecessary stress.

✦————————————————————————————✦

ESSENTIAL OILS

Spikenard

Spike lavender

Tulsi

Fir

Cistus

The Uranus-ruled essential oils are all helpful in the mental realm for clearing, soothing, grounding, removing stress or assisting with reaching higher levels of consciousness. As they work on minds and energetics, they are best used in a diffuser or oil burner, although you can dilute and apply them topically if you feel drawn to do so.

SPIKENARD creates balance and is used to reduce stress. SPIKE LAVENDER also traditionally soothes stress and relieves headaches – perfect for the frayed nerves from which Uranians can suffer.

TULSI (holy basil) is calming and clears the overthinking, wired or overtired mind.

FIR releases stress and frustration, clearing the air and removing the fog.

CISTUS is an excellent meditation companion, opening consciousness and enhancing feeling, while keeping your energetics grounded.

HEALING HERBS

Coffee

Kola nut

Guarana

Cacao

Tulsi

Altering consciousness, assisting higher mental faculties, balancing the mind and supporting the nervous system are the aims of Uranus's herbal friends. Uranus is an electrifying planet in terms of the nerves and brain, and it increases cognitive activity. It makes sense, therefore, that many of the Uranian herbs are highly stimulating, while others are nurturing, pacifying and balancing.

COFFEE, KOLA NUT and GUARANA are extremely stimulating. They sharpen the mind and increase mental ability (although too much can trigger anxiety, so keep the dose low).

CACAO raises consciousness, opening you up to inspiration and bringing about gentle alterations in the speed and clarity of your thinking.

TULSI (holy basil) is a tonic herb that acts as a mellowing balancer for the nervous system and will help you cope with stress.

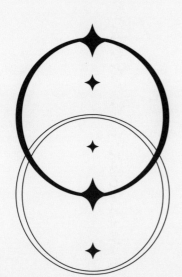

KINDRED ASSOCIATES

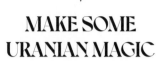

MAKE SOME URANIAN MAGIC

Meditate. Uranus provides the ability to access heightened levels of consciousness; meditation is the perfect way to make that possible.

Train your brain with puzzles and new games.

Express your individuality through your appearance. Uranus has a very punk vibe.

Wear some bright or light blue and feel that brilliant, illuminating energy.

FEELING UNBALANCED?

Ground yourself by walking barefoot on the Earth.

Temper your spacey energy with some body work, or get a massage or have acupuncture.

Eat some wholesome homemade comfort food and enjoy the cosiness.

NEEDING INSPIRATION?

Read about unique and inventive people to fuel your fire for what is possible in life.

Go wild with your visions and imagination; immediately write down what comes, so that you don't forget.

Learn about something that has always interested you and isn't related to your working life.

Break the rules and do something in your own – completely unique – way.

URANUS MEDITATION

FOR CENTRING YOURSELF

This is an active breathing meditation, as the energy of Uranus is full of thought and not particularly good at staying still. Anyone can use this breathing meditation – it is perfect for whenever you're feeling overstimulated and need to bring yourself back into balance. Because you have to focus on breathing, and counting the breath, you don't have much space to think, so it quietens the mind. Your nervous system benefits from stabilising your breathing into a repetitive pattern.

MEDITATION

Do this practice whenever you need to quickly ground yourself. It is ideal as a mini break – one quick minute if you feel a rush of stress coming on and need a fast reset. You could do it for up to ten minutes if the time is available to you (using a timer helps). This breath is known as the square breath and has an affinity with the number 4 (I like to do this for four minutes at a time). Your mind and energy will be clearer after this meditation. Try to breathe into the abdomen rather than the top of your chest, to experience a fuller level of groundedness.

Sit on a chair or cross-legged in a comfortable position but with a straight posture. Place your hands, palms down, on your knees. You can keep your eyes open or close them (I find closed eyes makes it easier to maintain my focus).

Take one long, slow, gentle breath in and out, letting all the breath out but not forcing or pushing.

Inhale for a slow count:

one, two, three, four.

Gently hold that breath in for a slow count:

one, two, three, four.

Exhale for a slow count:

one, two, three, four.

Gently hold that breath out for a slow count: one, two, three, four.

Continue to repeat this breath pattern until your timer rings or you feel it's time to end.

Take a final long, slow, gentle breath in and out, then gently get up again and enjoy the calm feeling.

MERCURY

INTELLECTUAL ✦ **COMMUNICATOR** ✦ *TEACHER*

THE NUMBER 5

✦✦✦

The number 5 relates to us in very special ways. We have five digits on each hand, five toes on each foot and possess the five senses of touch, taste, smell, vision and hearing. Pythagorean numerologists consider 5 to be the number of human life and to represent the marriage of the masculine and feminine principles. The number 5 also represents the head, arms and legs, considered to be the five appendages of the human body. If you lay out a person with their arms and legs outstretched, like Leonardo da Vinci's Vitruvian Man, the hands, feet and head mark the five points of the pentagram.

The pentagram is the number 5 embodied as a geometric shape. Pentagrams are a visual representation of the five elements of earth, fire, water, air and ether. Ether (also often called space) is the fifth element and is both unseen and unquantifiable. Ether represents space, divinity and the invisible spiritual energies of life. The pentagram is one of the most ancient of symbols and is significant in many religious faiths, although it is now a highly misunderstood design. The Christian faith used this symbol a long time ago, but nowadays they associate it with the Devil because of its importance to the Wiccan and Pagan movements.

In numerology, 5 carries many meanings, such as dynamism, changeability, curiosity, adventure, thought, attainment, learning and freedom. It is the central number – 5 sits smack bang in the middle of the single-digit numbers. Balance is important for the number 5 – it represents the harmony found at the middle point. The balancing point is always difficult to achieve and maintain, therefore people with 5 in their numerology must always strive for equilibrium as they can easily become unbalanced.

MERCURY

✦✦✦

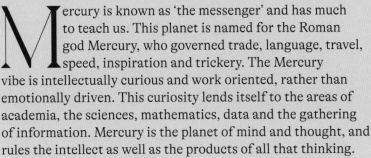

Mercury is known as 'the messenger' and has much to teach us. This planet is named for the Roman god Mercury, who governed trade, language, travel, speed, inspiration and trickery. The Mercury vibe is intellectually curious and work oriented, rather than emotionally driven. This curiosity lends itself to the areas of academia, the sciences, mathematics, data and the gathering of information. Mercury is the planet of mind and thought, and rules the intellect as well as the products of all that thinking.

Mercury is the planet that sits closest to the Sun in our solar system. It orbits the Sun in an unusual pattern and at a swift pace, taking only eighty-eight days to complete a full turn. It is also the smallest planet – just a third of the size of Earth and only slightly larger than our Moon. Mercury travels light, with no moons or rings to weigh it down – this planet doesn't do baggage. It is difficult to discover much about Mercury, as exploration is hampered by its exosphere and extreme temperatures. In 2004 NASA sent a robotic space probe – aptly named Messenger – on a ten-year discovery mission to Mercury; in March 2011 it became the first spacecraft to enter Mercury's orbit.

The word is Mercury's domain: everything word related is Mercury related. Writing (both factual and fictional), speaking and journalism are all Mercurial, as is anything to do with messaging, such as texts, email, copywriting, marketing, Morse code and other cyphers, phone calls and online messaging services. Language and interpretation between cultures is also governed by the chatty planet. Travel, as well: the journey, the experience and the learning that comes with travel are all in this planet's jurisdiction. All the different methods of travel – from planes, trains and automobiles, to boats and bikes – are also included in the Mercury zone.

5

✦

MERCURY FOUNDATION

◆————————————————◆

DAY
OF THE
WEEK
YOU
WERE
BORN

=

WEDNESDAY

5

MERCURY

FOUNDATION ◆ DAY OF THE WEEK YOU WERE BORN = WEDNESDAY

Those born on a Wednesday have a razor-sharp mind and wit. Ever the seeker of knowledge and wisdom, the Mercury foundation person has a huge appetite for learning, discovering and analysing. With a high intellectual capacity and an ambition for knowledge, you succeed in everything you desire to master. Your quicksilver speed is a gift – in conversation, grasping concepts and communicating. The Mercury foundation has a lot to say and you might either be an extremely fast talker, or be overwhelmed by all the things in your mind and confuse your listener, or even not say much at all.

Usually, however, you will be an exceptionally skilled, nimble and clever communicator with a real talent when it comes to words. The gift of the gab is definitely your thing. Anything word related is in Mercury's domain and this can manifest in a multitude of ways. You might excel at the written or spoken word: to call you 'eloquent' is an understatement. Mercury people are very aware of the power of words, which they can use for good or not-so-good purposes. There is, of course, a manipulative Mercurial type who uses their silver tongue to get what they want out of people or have others believe what they want them to believe. Some Mercuries can be a little slippery that way, but it's always far better for you to use your powers for good.

Share your wisdom, love and inspiration through words: they are your magic and your gift. Remember, words are spells, so speak and write them with absolute care to see the best possible outcomes reflected in your world. You can truly create with this power. Linguistics are powerful for you and you have a natural talent for picking up other languages. Mercuries seek to not only know the facts, but also to understand every aspect. Diplomacy is another talent. Some might say the Mercury is two-faced, or sits on the fence instead of choosing sides, but the reality is that they usually just want to comprehend both sides of any story. You look for the truth and also for the other truth, the other potentials, the other perspective.

156

Mercurial people are attracted to philosophy like bees to flowers. You love to intellectualise, conceptualise and theorise. The pursuit of learning is your lifelong goal and you love to be experiencing as well as living in your head. Your love of travel is more than just ticking off places on a list: you want to immerse yourself in the culture of a place and really understand it. You enjoy connecting with different people, different places and different ways of living. You must get out and about in the world and discover life from different perspectives – it's important you don't hole yourself up with your pursuits and cut yourself off from people and experiences.

Anxiety is the curse of the Mercury mind and you can tend towards being a worry wart. Stress can easily get to you and this will affect your overall wellbeing more than it does most other people. Mercuries put a lot of pressure on themselves and have a tendency to be extra self-critical and self-demanding, with very high expectations. Those expectations apply to the self but can spill onto other people in your life, so take care not to be too critical or to have unrealistic expectations of perfection, for yourself and for others. You might also have a tendency to shut out the world and focus solely on your pet pursuits, which can affect your social and personal life. The people around you could feel you are unemotional. It's not that you don't feel, it's more that you keep your feelings hidden, have a hard time articulating them, or are mentally dwelling in your own dimension.

Mercuries excel at academia and all forms of study. You make fantastic experts and specialists with your high-achiever streak and will push yourself to be as educated as possible on the subjects you're interested in. Being naturally curious, Mercuries are frequently polymaths, into many and varied subjects and highly knowledgeable and skilled in all of them. The Mercury foundation can become an expert on anything they choose to learn about, and more quickly than other people because they are fast learners with great memories.

5

✦

MERCURY

You tend to have a lot of nervous energy and always be in motion, even a little frenetic. It's best to keep yourself occupied, so that you don't become too restless. Be a lifelong student and indulge your desire to discover, to know, to cultivate wisdom. Travel is a must – even if it's not to foreign lands, you need to explore other places and escape your usual routine. Philosophise, discuss and share ideas with other smart people; stimulating conversation is spiritual sustenance for the Mercury. Find ways to relax that work for you and are easy to maintain consistently in your life. Stress is a massive downer for you and must be carefully managed.

5

✦

MERCURY PERSONALITY

✦————————————✦

DAY
OF THE
MONTH
YOU
WERE
BORN
=
5

MER
CU
RY

The Mercury personality bestows on you an innately inquisitive and analytical nature with a tendency to think very deeply. Mercury in this placement makes a person more hesitant to take risks without thinking things through and inspecting the situation from all angles. Nothing gets by you; you like to scrutinise the details thoroughly. If and when you do get carried away, though, you can be a bit careless and forget to dot the i's and cross the t's. Not because you are negligent but because, when you immerse yourself in something, you *really* immerse and can become obsessed to the exclusion of all else. This honing ability is a great skill at other times, though, helping Mercuries become specialists in any field.

Versatile, adaptive and agile, the Mercury personality is the most fluid of the placements. You can go with the flow and are always open-minded, preferring to explore all potentials and possibilities rather than be stuck in any one position. Mercury is known to be mutable and changeable, open to interpretation and open to evolving. This trait makes you a great team player – collaborative, cooperative and keen to find the best solution for the benefit of the group. Other people love that about you; they also love your amusing conversation, astute observations and brilliant sense of humour. Beware the kind of intellectual snobbery that isolates a person – mix with all kinds and remember to truly listen. It's amazing what you can pick up from other people when you pay attention.

The Mercury personality is in continual motion and doesn't like to feel weighed down. You aren't dispassionate about or unaware of the state of the world, but you are more attuned to the fun end of the spectrum and prefer to live a life of possibility rather than feel hopeless or paralysed by negativity. You are a realist but you want to enjoy life, too. This can seem frivolous to more serious types, but your Mercury personality isn't light in a vacuous sense; you just like to keep moving along and will change the subject if things get boring or depressing.

Mercury in this placement makes for a pragmatic person, more stoic than sensitive, preferring to move forwards and leave the past where it belongs. Impatience is an issue for the Mercury personality: you don't like to sit around doing nothing, and hate waiting for anything or anyone. If you have Mercury in this placement, you need to get used to the fact that other people are not as fast-paced as you are and can't get as much done in the same amount of time. You will only be still when you have completely exhausted yourself, mentally and often physically. However, this constant doing can lead to nervous exhaustion and make you moody, so if you find yourself snappy and impatient then it's time to slow down.

Mercury is the planet of the merchant and rules all things trade related. Suffice to say, you are blessed with excellent business skills. Sales and winning deals and contracts gives you a great buzz; you love the sense of achievement that comes from raking in the cash. You are very thorough and meticulous when it comes to your work and will put in the effort and hours required to excel. You can be one-track minded, so keep your communication inclusive at work. Many Mercury personalities could be described as absolute workaholics. Although you can definitely climb the ladders and achieve major goals, don't ever forget there is more to life than work. No one's dying wish is ever, 'I wish I'd put in more hours at the office'.

Thinking, thinking and more thinking is the Mercury speciality. 'I think, therefore I am' is the Mercury personality motto and it's all too easy to live inside your mind full-time. To bring out the best of this placement, balance your intense intellectual and career activity with the sensory world. Find ways to fully occupy your body beyond the head zone and allow yourself to feel as well as think. Follow the life paths that make you passionate and fascinated, otherwise you'll be unhappy and create trouble for yourself just to keep things interesting. It's important for a Mercury personality to love what they do for a living, as that's what they put the most energy into.

5

✦

MERCURY DESTINY

✦ ———————————————————————— ✦

DAY

+

MONTH

+

YEAR

=

5

MER CU RY

Those with a Mercury destiny have a message to deliver to the world. You are naturally driven to be the best and excel in your field of expertise – you might even have a few different fields of expertise in your life. A dedicated and gifted student, you study to gain wisdom and learn, rather than for career gain. To know and understand is where you find joy. You revel in the details and love to discover the intricacies and finer points of a subject. It is good for you to continue to stretch your intellectual legs as you go through life.

Mercuries are excellent problem solvers – when they care about the outcome – and are constantly working to find the angle that hasn't yet been considered. The Mercury destiny is able to fine-tune, to hone in on the details, to analyse and dissect the situation at hand. This is fantastic when there is a problem to be dealt with, but not ideal when there isn't one. When this is your destiny planet, you must be aware of your tendency to overthink and overanalyse or worry excessively. With nothing to stress over, you can become bored and look for problems where there aren't any, simply to give yourself something to solve. Better to channel that into learning, exploring and work.

Light on your feet, the Mercury destiny likes to also travel light through life. You aren't hugely possession oriented (although you might be an avid collector). There is a fastness that is always present: even if you appear to be still, you are likely to be going a million miles an hour in your head. 'Eccentric' is a word that often comes up around Mercury people, and you do like to go your own way and do your own thing. Mercuries won't commit to anything unless they are all-in, body, heart and mind. If you are into something, you want to know everything. Mercury destinies are the specialisation people, the experts and authorities. Skill honing to the point of becoming a master craftsperson or leader in your field is the ideal outcome for your interests.

Mercury destinies can become great at anything they choose; however, some particularly suitable careers are teaching (in any capacity), the sciences, business, economics, finance, mathematics (Mercuries often have a talent for numbers), retail, sales, travel, communications, writing and academia. Being a business owner, manager or head of department is ideal because of your need for freedom and your desire to do things your own way. Mercuries are inventive, innovative, specific and exacting, and great in roles where they have to use their brains to come up with something new or better.

Skill honing to the point of becoming a master craftsperson or leader in your field is the ideal outcome for your interests.

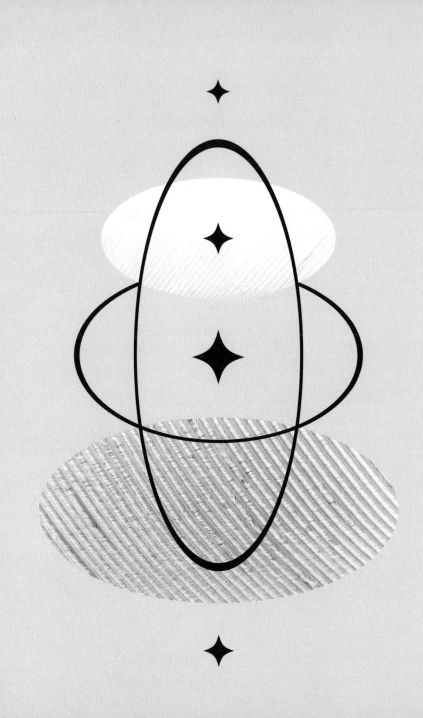

5

✦

MERCURY RELATIONSHIPS

✦————————————————————✦

YOUR
DESTINY
NUMBER
+
THEIR
DESTINY
NUMBER
=
5

MERCURY

Talk, converse, commune, consult and connect. The discourse is what this alliance is all about. Focus on the spoken and written dialogue. Choose your words with care – they are extra important and have the greatest impact in this relationship. Words can enhance, strengthen, uplift and bring this connection closer. They can also create distance, hurt feelings and bring it right down. The Mercury relationship can truly be your greatest teacher, so it's important to pay attention to it. Listen to the other and be ready to learn from them. Mercury is a changeable planet, so the best advice for anyone in a Mercury relationship is to allow the evolution of the other person and yourself to take place. Let this relationship alter you and show you other ways of being.

Mercury connections are lively, fun and intellectually stimulating, with never a dull moment! This is the ideal travel companion scenario: you explore well together and, in fact, anything that takes both of you out of the familiar and gives you something to talk about infuses this relationship with maximum happiness. Sort out any miscommunications as soon as they pop up and be willing to see both sides of any story. Being set in your ways or stuck in your opinions won't be helpful in this relationship. Learning together, travelling together, discovering together and doing business together are all given a boost by Mercury. The interaction between the two of you will make each of you a wiser person. Work this dynamic by approaching the relationship as a way of knowing each other – and yourself – better.

The Mercurial love relationship is an interesting fish, being very much a meeting of minds and more about the journey than the destination. Mercury the planet blows hot and cold, and so can this relationship. Enjoy the shifting winds and adapt, rather than trying to box it in. It can be difficult to get to the full commitment stage with this one, not because of lack of love but because there is still so much to explore together before settling down. Mercury romances often stay young for a long time in the sense that they avoid sameness and maintain their variety for longer. The Mercury love match must keep things creative and interesting and not become mired in how the conventions dictate a love partnership should look. Let the relationship breathe. Let it be what it is. You learn together – this is an exciting and highly valuable prize.

Listen to the other and be ready to learn from them. Mercury is a changeable planet, so the best advice for anyone in a Mercury relationship is to allow the evolution of the other person and yourself to take place.

KINDRED MERCURY ASSOCIATES

These are the special friends of Mercury, connected and aligned with the quirky, quicksilver energy of this lively planet. They embody Mercurial characteristics and can be called upon to support or enhance your Mercury energy, whether or not this is one of your planets. Use this information and work with Mercury to balance, inspire, heal and make magic happen.

MERCURY

POWER COLOUR

YELLOW

Yellow is the Mercury colour and relates to changeability, communication, memory, enthusiasm, playfulness, wit and intelligence. Yellow has many different – and sometimes contradictory – associations, such as cheerfulness, life force and energy as well as illness, jealousy and warning. This is an indication that its mutability matches the energy of Mercury.

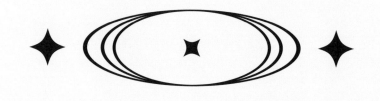

POWER DAY

WEDNESDAY

Wednesday is ruled by Mercury and known as Mercury day in many languages. Wednesday was originally *Wodensdag*, after the Germanic god Woden (Odin in Norse), who was known as a god of wisdom, thought, memory, learning, battle, poetry and magic. Communicate, communicate, communicate on a Wednesday. Infuse your expression with wit and charm to bring others on side.

Send that email, put in that application, make that request and give that presentation. Mercury is the messenger, so be clear about what you are sending to avoid mixed messages. Words have extra power today: use them wisely and for good. Remember to breathe, hydrate and eat well as you go about your day. Mercury moves fast and gets caught up in the moment, forgetting basic needs.

ASTROLOGICAL SIGNS

GEMINI AND VIRGO

ELEMENT

AIR

Mercury is associated with the very airy qualities of thought, the mind, intelligence, changeability and mobility.

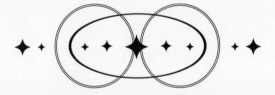

TAROT CARDS

The cards of the Hierophant and Temperance are numbered 5 and 14 in the major arcana of the tarot, with 14 becoming 5 when you add 1 + 4. If you are looking into the tarot or doing tarot spreads, be aware that these cards are associated with the energy of 5 and Mercury. They express Mercurial concepts, such as knowledge, learning, educating, creative problem solving, finding equilibrium, stress in the mind, the need to stay grounded and the cultivating of patience.

BODY NURTURE ZONES

Mercury governs the nervous system, five senses, thyroid, respiratory system and hormones (the messengers of the body). All things to do with our brain and mental health are this planet's focus. The thyroid is our communication centre, energetically speaking. Less obvious is the respiratory system; however, consider how inspiration (the intake of breath or inspiration that comes to the mind) is so Mercury, as is talking, for which we need lungs. Mercuries should reduce stress and sensory overload, get plenty of sleep and breathe well.

✦ ─────────────────────── ✦

ESSENTIAL OILS

Peppermint

Eucalyptus

Bergamot

Geranium

Sweet marjoram

Mercuries respond well to aromatics, although you often have a highly responsive sense of smell, so be careful with the amounts.

PEPPERMINT is a refreshing head clearer and a famous aid for tension headaches.

EUCALYPTUS opens and clears the airways. It's perfect for respiratory issues, and for cleansing a mind that is stuck in a negative rut.

BERGAMOT is a balancer with the Mercury talent for blending. It goes well with most other essential oils and calms the nervous system.

GERANIUM is a balancing, comforting oil, and the perfect aromatic for Mercuries who need to lighten up.

SWEET MARJORAM soothes the nerves, calms an overly active mind and helps the restless sleeper.

HEALING HERBS

Ginkgo biloba

Brahmi

Gotu kola

Licorice

Skullcap

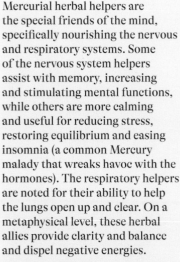

Mercurial herbal helpers are the special friends of the mind, specifically nourishing the nervous and respiratory systems. Some of the nervous system helpers assist with memory, increasing and stimulating mental functions, while others are more calming and useful for reducing stress, restoring equilibrium and easing insomnia (a common Mercury malady that wreaks havoc with the hormones). The respiratory helpers are noted for their ability to help the lungs open up and clear. On a metaphysical level, these herbal allies provide clarity and balance and dispel negative energies.

GINKGO BILOBA, BRAHMI and GOTU KOLA awaken the mind and are traditionally considered to increase mental capacity and enhance cognitive performance. Brahmi and gotu kola are also tonics to the nervous system, giving strength and assisting it to cope with the effects of stress.

LICORICE is considered a balancing herb and known to be excellent for soothing a cough. It is also used by herbalists for those suffering stress and exhaustion.

SKULLCAP is calming and sedating for the nervous system and a traditional go-to remedy for stress headaches, insomnia and anxiety.

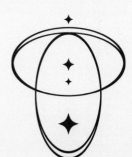

MAKE SOME MERCURIAL MAGIC

Write down your daily thoughts and experiences. Keeping a journal is highly Mercurial.

Get out of your neighbourhood, even if it's only to a new suburb or town.

Discuss philosophy and the meaning of life with other interested people.

NEEDING INSPIRATION?

Plan your next trip. List all the places you want to go to and things you want to see and experience.

Thrill your senses with a gastronomic adventure at a fancy restaurant.

Learn a new language, study another culture or sign up for a course. Your inner academic lives to learn.

Seek out people who are interested in the same areas as you, so you can enjoy being nerdy together!

FEELING UNBALANCED?

Breathe. Mercuries often get so caught up in their thoughts they forget themselves. Stop, inhale and exhale fully and deeply to reset.

Your mind is connected to the physical form and staying grounded is a must. take a walk to get back into your body.

Remove unnecessary distractions from your day, so you can focus on the stuff that matters.

MERCURY MEDITATION

FOR MENTAL CLARITY

✦
|
✦

This meditation ritual is all about emptying out an overactive or upset mind. Anyone can do this and it's the perfect solution for when your headspace is overly full, overloaded with stress, or stuck in a thought loop you want to escape. This practice can also be used to help you come up with solutions to problems. When you clear the clutter in your head, the answers will come through much more easily. All you need is paper and something to write with.

Find a quiet place or cosy corner where you
won't be disturbed by other people.

Grab your writing implement and paper and write, entirely from
your stream of consciousness. Write everything that comes to your
mind, no matter how strange or absurd it is. Don't worry about
spelling or grammar or your messy handwriting – no one else is ever
going to see it.

When you feel as if you've got everything out of your system and
your mind is serene again, stop writing.

Rip up your paper ramblings and throw them away.

VENUS

LOVER ✦ AESTHETE ✦ FRIEND

THE NUMBER 6

✦✦✦

In mathematics, 6 is considered a perfect number because when you add or multiply the first three numbers (1, 2 and 3) the answer is 6: 1 + 2 + 3 = 6, and 1 × 2 × 3 = 6. The number 6 in numerology is traditionally considered the number of harmony and marriage. Balance, union and equality are what 6 aims to teach us. The hexagram is the six-pointed star (made up of two interlocking triangles, one pointing up, the other pointing down) and the hexagon is a six-sided geometric shape. Both of these shapes are comprised of equal parts, and at the centre of the hexagram you find the hexagon shape. The hexagram unites the masculine and feminine principles, and those of fire and water. The text of the ancient book of Chinese divination *I Ching* consists of sixty-four 'hexagrams' – in this case, characters composed of six stacked lines (either broken or complete) – and their meanings.

Creation is also one of the meanings of the number 6. The six days of God's working to make heaven and Earth in the Bible is just one of many creation mythologies around this number. Speaking of the Bible, many an aversion to 6 has stemmed from triple 6 being the number of the beast. In numerology, though, this number actually adds to 9 (because 6 + 6 + 6 = 18, and 18 is further reduced by adding 1 + 8 = 9). The number 9 is ruled by Mars and requires conscious control over our baser impulses, which makes more sense overall. However, because 6 is the number of union, it also represents sex – so might cause disapproval for other reasons!

Creativity as a concept and an act (yes, we're talking about sex in all its earthly forms) is aligned with the energy of 6. Interaction and interplay are key themes. To create, we must interact – with others, our surroundings and aspects of ourselves. Family – chosen and inherited – is also connected to 6, and we seek the balance and harmony of 6 in our family life.

VENUS

✦✦✦

Venus is the brightest and hottest planet in the solar system. It is roughly the same size as Earth and often called Earth's 'twin', although the differences between the two planets far outweigh that one similarity. Venus is covered in a thick smoggy atmosphere and has an air pressure that makes it impossible for human survival – it's similar to being a kilometre underwater. Plenty of spacecraft have explored its outer atmosphere, though – it was the first planet to be 'flown by', scanned and mapped by NASA in 1962.

Venus is so bright that, like the Moon, it can at times be seen during daytime. It is called the morning or evening star because, like the Sun, it can be seen to rise like a giant sparkle in the morning and set in the evening. Named for the Roman goddess of love, sex, desire, fertility and beauty, Venus is the planetary inspiration of lovers, artists, sensualists and creatives. In the classical Roman myth, Venus was married to Vulcan, the god of fire and blacksmiths, but couldn't resist a sexy fling with passionate Mars (although Mars wasn't the only god and man reputed to have fallen for the considerable charms of Venus).

Everyone knows Venus as the planet of love, but Venus is so much more than that. All things harmony and beauty are in its domain: poetry, friendship, design, works of art, mouthfuls of deliciousness, flowers, music, self-adornment, craftsmanship and well-decorated spaces are so Venusian. Attraction is also a Venus speciality. The attraction between two (or more) people is an obvious conclusion to jump to; however, the principle of attraction can be applied to many other scenarios. Venus represents putting your best self across, going out into the world and seeking to attract what you are attracted to on a bigger scale. Just as you would get ready and head out to meet a potential lover, so you can also get ready and head out to meet other desired destinies.

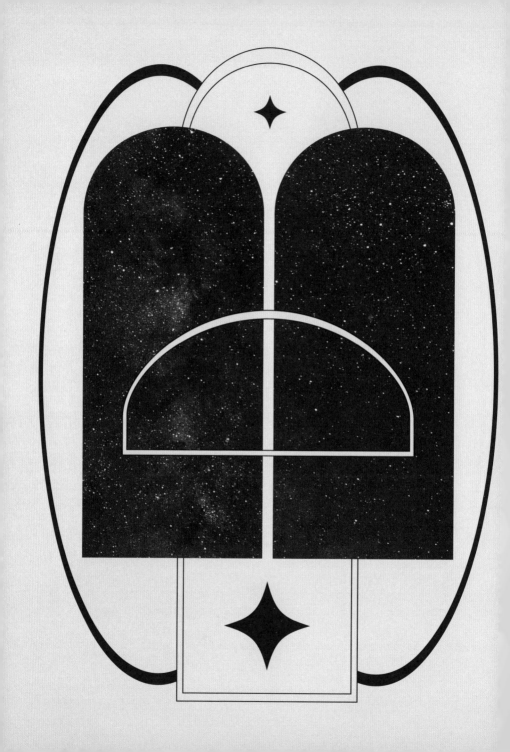

6

✦

VENUS FOUNDATION

✦ —————————————— ✦

DAY
OF THE
WEEK
YOU
WERE
BORN

=

FRIDAY

The Friday-born beauty is Venus on legs. A Venus foundation is always a captivating presence to be around. You ooze charm and are socially aware, elegant, beautiful, fun and excellent company. A Venus can bring any person out of their shell and, when you give your attention, that person will bloom and open like a flower. Venus foundations come into their own at social occasions and gatherings, making sure everyone is having a good time. You will either be the life of the party or the glue smoothly holding it all together. Even the shy Venus, who's more of an introvert, will possess brilliant hospitality instincts and the ability to make sure everyone is well looked after.

One of your talents is being able to connect with others and make them feel good. As Maya Angelou famously said, 'People will never forget how you made them feel,' and a Venus knows it. You go out of your way to make other people feel positively about you, and you worry excessively if you think you've made a bad impression. Killing people with kindness is a Venusian art form. You love to chat, flirt, laugh, schmooze and mingle, and you know how to have a good time and enjoy yourself. You make friends with ease, your people skills are second to none and working this magic into your life can help you succeed in many ways.

Because of your Venusian interpersonal skills, admirers are not hard to come by and many people will be attracted to your brightness. People crush on Venus constantly, probably more than you realise. You are naturally friendly and easy to be around; others could misinterpret that as romantic interest from you, so be sure to mention you are attached if you are, so that no one gets the wrong idea. Be aware that your powers of flirtation and seduction are extraordinarily strong; use them wisely, or you can end up creating confusion and drama in your love life. Save your flirt factor for when you really mean it.

Beauty is a big part of who you are, and this goes way beyond the basic level of personal grooming and hygiene. Although Venus foundations are dreamboats who typically look great with seemingly minimal effort, they have a highly developed eye for all things beautiful. Venus foundations radiate beauty, relate to it, crave, imbibe, savour and collect it – you enjoy beautiful art, styling, music, writing, design, fine food, wine and people. If it's gorgeous and well made, you will appreciate it. Venusians are connoisseurs.

Venus is highly creative, and you will be naturally good at anything to do with art and design, as well as anything requiring a flourish of good taste or a little bit of surprise and delight. Creative thinking is another gift: you are able to hold a vision for unique ways to do things, especially when that involves creating a more harmonious or aesthetically pleasing outcome. Quality is highly important and everything you do has to be of the highest calibre. This quality control also applies to what Venus foundations wear, eat, drink and surround themselves with. The love of luxury is a famous Venus attribute and, for the foundation placement, this manifests in the desire for perfection, often relating to what they produce at work and what they create. For some, it's in how they look (which can be very stressful and unhelpful).

Those with this planet as their foundation are the tastemakers of the world, possessing an enviable and highly specific style and remarkable creative abilities. Other people might imitate you, which is annoying, but try to see it as a sign of your excellence. Speaking of that perfectionist streak, many with this placement feel any imperfections, no matter how small, make them unlovable. Perfectionism can create much disharmony in your life. Venus foundations commonly feel nothing they do is ever good enough and that they are fundamentally inadequate. Know this: you are just as worthy as every other perfectly imperfect human. Perfection is not a prerequisite for love.

Emotional neediness is a bit of a Venus thing, and a lot of your self-image can be too caught up in your connections with other people. You are also highly sensitive to anything resembling criticism, either real or imagined. Provide yourself with only some of what you need from relationships, as well as receiving some from your loved ones, because being emotionally self-reliant feels so much better, and makes for healthier relationships in general. When it comes to love specifically, do not enter relationships with the expectation that the other person will make you feel 'complete' and 'whole'. No one can do that but you. Idealism is often mixed up in our love lives and for the Venus foundation this is especially pronounced. Rely on yourself and other close people for emotional sustenance, too, so that you're not dependent on just one person.

To bring out the best in this Venus placement, work on valuing yourself regardless of how you appear to others. Nourish your self-worth by celebrating all the good you have done and can do. Create and keep healthy emotional boundaries and work on your relationship with yourself. Establish and maintain deep and meaningful connections with others: it's far better to have a few true friends than a gaggle of groupies, fakes and fawners hanging around. Enjoy, and be inspired by, the finer, high-quality and beautiful things in life. Abolish perfectionism and accept things the way they are – yes, you absolutely can strive for the best, but don't make achieving it the be all and end all. Let your inner artist out to play. Allow yourself daily fun.

6

✦

VENUS PERSONALITY

◆————————————————————◆

DAY
OF THE
MONTH
YOU
WERE
BORN

=

6

Sensuality is the calling card of the Venus personality. All the delicious things are in your domain and you are the ruler of having a good time. The Venus senses are finely tuned and highly sensitive, all the better to enjoy the delights on offer. Tactile and warm, you love to connect and love physical touch. People are drawn to your sweet personality and respond well to your energy. They enjoy being around you, which makes you excellent in any person-to-person situation. You have the ability to smooth and harmonise your surroundings, including whoever is inhabiting the space. People-centred careers are often where the Venus personality can be found.

The Venus home is the land of good food and drinks, convivial gatherings and scintillating conversation. It is *the* place to go for emotional support and fun with friends. Beautiful environs are a speciality, and your home sanctuary is both a sacred space for you and yours and a natural extension of your personal style. Venus personalities have the remarkable ability to make anywhere feel like home and beautify any place. People are instinctively at ease and comfortable in your presence. These talents are useful outside the home in everyday life, especially in the workplace, where your bright demeanour can easily elevate the whole place.

Family and children are often very important to the Venus personality and this might manifest in different ways. Some will have babies aplenty; others parent in other ways, with animals, adoption and fostering, being the cool auntie or uncle, or taking care of plant collections. The fertility of your Venus personality is also easily channelled into other forms of creativity – you don't have to produce fruit from your loins to be fertile in your life. Family-wise, too, you might be very close to your biological family or have a gorgeous chosen family that you amass over your lifetime.

Venus loves love. Some might call you a hopeless romantic, but believing in the power of love is a gift. Marriage or long-term partnerships are your thing, but it can be difficult to find that needle in the haystack. Your person *does* exist, although they might not be as perfect as you imagine, so stay realistic. The *idea* of someone can often be more interesting than the actual person. Special note to the lovelorn Venus: if someone exists only in your head and your inbox, and not really in your life for some overly complicated reason, then stop wasting your energy. Those who are genuinely present in your life and truly available to you are the ones to focus on. If the object of your desire is unavailable to you, be unavailable to them.

You are very particular style-wise; you know what you like and are very definitive about it. To Venus, life doesn't imitate art, it *is* art. Everything should be made to be as beautiful as it can be. You might have a tendency to care a bit too much about how things look and keeping up appearances. Beware this trap. You are enough as you are and your life is enough as it is. Of course, things can always be improved upon, but the more you appreciate who you are and what you have, the happier you will be. Finding fulfilment where you are is something you can master when you let go of idealism and escape the perfectionism prison.

Another gift you possess is that of being highly intuitive with people, especially emotionally. With Venus in this placement, if you choose to tune in, you can sense what others are feeling. Your emotional intelligence is greater than most and, when you work on this, you can experience fantastic rapport and connection with others.

If you feel emotionally empty, you will be tempted to fill that gap with lovely objects, food or sex. This feels good at the time but won't work for you in the long run. It's better to let yourself feel some emotional pain and be done with it than bypass it and pay later. Don't avoid difficult conversations for the sake of maintaining a veneer of everything being peachy. You can be honest about your feelings without overindulging them or being ruled by emotion.

6

✦

VENUS DESTINY

✦————————————————————✦

DAY

+

MONTH

+

YEAR

=

6

Venus destiny people are the harmonisers of the world, seeking and creating harmony wherever they go. You are adaptable with people and can get along with most, which serves you very well in life. Don't be afraid to petition for favours or ask for what you want; most of the time you will find that people want to give it to you. Your charm is your biggest asset. People find you easy to like and love because you *are* easy to like and love. You possess grace – a rare and valuable quality.

Emotional balance and fulfilment is one of your tasks in life, and something to be conscious of working towards at all times. You feel very deeply (although you might not show it at all) and are very sensitive to everything around you, in particular the reactions and behaviours of other people towards you. Be sure to be with people who love you for who you are and support you on an emotional level (or at least try to do so). Your tastes are refined and you possess a natural elegance. Usually Venus likes simplicity, although some Venus destinies love a bit of embellishment, boldness and flash and have a 'more is more' aesthetic. Be wary of a tendency for frivolity; be careful not to overspend.

To the Venus destiny, sex is important, magically transformative and ultra healing when it's with the right person or people. On the flipside, sex can become the bane of your existence, causing you all sorts of trouble. It's vital that you maintain a healthy sex life and have balance in this area. Make sure your sexual interactions are emotionally safe and loving, with people you can trust. Absolutely avoid any sort of love triangle (unless you are all happy with and fully aware of the entire scenario). Higher love is where it's really at, and when you connect love to something greater than human relations, this is where you can find more fulfilment.

The talents and skills of the Venus destiny, and the areas where their gifts really shine, are anything to do with the arts, design and creative industries. Your personality and style-icon vibe is highly suited to these areas. Fashion is another world that lures Venuses, and anything in this realm suits. You will have lots of success in areas such as marketing, PR, advertising, sales and events, where your sterling people skills come out to play. Anything customer focused brings forth your charm-offensive talents. Luxury goods, perfumery, personal care and cosmetics are pure Venus, as is anything to do with flavour. Venus destinies do very well in the food and drinks business, especially when creating a convivial atmosphere is part of their role.

The talents and skills of the Venus destiny, and the areas where their gifts really shine, are anything to do with the arts, design and creative industries.

6

✦

VENUS RELATIONSHIPS

✦————————————————————✦

YOUR
DESTINY
NUMBER
+
THEIR
DESTINY
NUMBER
=
6

H armonious interaction is the cornerstone of the happy Venus relationship. Whether it's a love, family, friendship or work thing, the most important goal is to keep the union happening. Keeping things light and fun breathes fresh air into this alliance and allows for the kinds of experiences that turn into seriously happy memories. The emotional support is there, but ultimately this relationship is at its best when the two of you are enjoying being together. Bringing elements of celebration, pleasure and entertainment into the everyday is the grease that keeps the wheels of the Venus connection turning. Plenty of positive affirmation brings this connection into full bloom. It's vital for the Venusian vibration that love is poured on thick. Show that you care and let it rain praise.

This relationship is hugely sensitive to criticism, bad moods, temper flare-ups and careless words. What is needed is kindness, gentleness and consideration of each other's needs and feelings – a sort of mutual appreciation society! Because Venus loves the arts, anything creatively inspiring, such as going to music gigs or festivals, the cinema, art galleries and the theatre, is an ideal bonding activity. The same goes for anything celebratory, such as a party, event or even just getting dressed up to go out. Fun is absolutely essential. Because of the famous Venus perfectionist streak, do work on your unrealistic expectations of yourself and the other. Appreciate them for who they are and don't nit-pick.

The Venusian love relationship can truly be the most sumptuously romantic of all the unions. This bond can feel very starry-eyed, especially in the early stages. It's the kind of love that can age like those gorgeous old couples who still romance each other after forty years, or, like Romeo and Juliet, can end in a flurry of dramatic, overblown, possibly hormone-driven hysteria. Keep your nerve and maintain your sense of self, as full-on enmeshment can easily happen with a Venus love pairing. Aside from that warning, the only other thing to watch out for is your unrealistic expectations undermining the depth of what is actually there. Don't put another human on a pedestal or you'll invite inevitable disappointment. Work to keep the courtship, flirtation, sexual generosity and spontaneity alive. Love each other with wide-open hearts, give generously of your love, express and demonstrate how much you care, and this relationship can be heavenly.

Bringing elements of celebration, pleasure and entertainment into the everyday is the grease that keeps the wheels of the Venus connection turning.

KINDRED VENUS ASSOCIATES

These are the special friends
and correspondences of Venus,
connected and aligned with the
harmonious and gorgeous energy
of this beautiful planet. They
embody Venusian characteristics
and can be called upon to
support or enhance your Venus
energy, whether or not this is
one of your planets. Use this
information and work with Venus
to balance, inspire, heal and
make magic happen.

POWER COLOURS

PINK AND GREEN

Pink is the colour most often associated with Venus. Pink is associated with love, flushing from sexual attraction, the feminine principle, gentleness, lightheartedness and friendship. Green is also frequently associated with Venus and the Venusian qualities of fertility, nature, creativity, harmony, springtime and love.

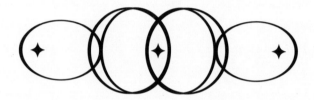

POWER DAY

FRIDAY

Friday was named after Frija, the Germanic goddess of love, beauty, fertility, marriage, magic, foresight and the finer things in life (Frigg is the Norse version). For people with Venus as one of their numerology planets, every Friday is extra special and supportive. Even if you don't have Venus as one of your planets, you can connect with these properties to have a more aligned day. Venus brings some much needed *va va voom* to the week and Friday is the perfect day for anything to do with art, design, beauty, connection and socialising. Venus loves love, so dating, seducing and maintaining romantic relationships is the perfect area into which to direct your Venusian energy. Definitely say yes to that enticing invitation! Put your best foot forward, and make sure it's wearing a fabulous shoe. Enjoy the good things in life. A little indulgence will up your joy factor.

ASTROLOGICAL SIGNS	ELEMENT

TAURUS AND LIBRA

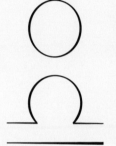

WATER

Water is traditionally associated with Venus, because the feminine principle is likened to water with its fluidity, reflection and capacity to receive. Water is the universal solvent. You can lose yourself in water, just as you can in Venus.

Earth is the other element associated with Venus and represents Venusian aspects of the material world, such as beauty, luxury, nature and the abundant sensual pleasures of life.

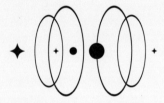

TAROT CARDS

The cards of the Lovers and the Devil are numbered 6 and 15 in the major arcana of the tarot, with 15 becoming 6 when you add 1 + 5. If you are doing a tarot reading or studying the cards, be aware that both these cards have a looming figure above the archetypal man and woman. They speak of the temptations of forbidden fruit, primal desires and the attraction between two lovers – all very Venusian. Although different in tone, both cards offer a lesson in overcoming being ruled by fickleness or base sexual impulses, and in rising above them.

BODY NURTURE ZONES

Venus governs the kidneys, sex organs and sexual desire, the skin and hair, and the heart in the emotional and energetic sense. With Venus as one of your planets, looking after your sexual and emotional health is vital. The pancreas is also a nurture zone, as overindulgence in sweet foods can be a Venus vice.

ESSENTIAL OILS

Rose

Rose geranium

Palmarosa

Ylang Ylang

Vanilla

Perfume is an art born of Venus, and these essential oils perfectly personify Venus in the form of scent. All the Venusian aromatics have calming properties. These oils can be diluted and applied topically to enhance your allure, or evaporated in oil burners or diffusers to create a mood.

ROSE is appreciated for its heart-resonating qualities. This precious oil helps us with learning to love the self – vital work for Venus people.

ROSE GERANIUM balances out the emotions. It has a fresh, spring-like aroma.

PALMAROSA soothes a stressed or lonely heart, and has a deep tea-like, rosy aroma which gently grounds the flightiness of Venus.

YLANG YLANG is a heady, sexual, narcotic aromatic that brings out the inner minx in anyone.

VANILLA has a sweet, yet rich and potent, scent that most people love – a great attractant to potential lovers.

HEALING HERBS

Honey

Rose

Yarrow

Damiana

Shatavari

Venusian herbs are usually either gently cooling or warming, and moistening to the body's tissues. The herbal friends of Venus are balancers, bringing harmony to the body. There are also herbs to enhance the sex drive, open the heart in the energetic sense, and some that act as a tonic to the body. They are often on the sweet side, as Venus rules that taste.

HONEY, although not a herb, is a Venusian natural medicine of note. Having been revered as an aphrodisiac since ancient times, it is deliciously sweet and boosts nitric oxide levels, which helps men's blood flow and erectile function.

ROSE energetically opens, softens and soothes the heart. It is calming and gentle and brings ease to stress and grief states, as well as supporting self-love.

YARROW is traditionally used as a gentle tonic herb. It was once believed that if you put yarrow under your pillow and recited a spell, you would dream of your future life partner.

DAMIANA is a famous aphrodisiac, while SHATAVARI, which can be translated as 'she with a hundred husbands', is a traditional tonic, both in the general and sexual sense.

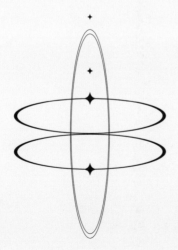

VE
N
US

MAKE SOME VENUSIAN MAGIC

For those not in a monogamous relationship, flirt like crazy and enjoy a little harmless banter with a cutie.

Dress up in your finest, groom yourself and go out. Or stay at home and enjoy your own fabulousness, for the fun of it.

Gather the people you like and love the most to create a beautiful shindig.

Get a new hairdo, manicure, body treatment or facial, or buy some delicious perfume to douse your sexy self in.

NEEDING INSPIRATION?

Journal about your feelings, impressions, love life and sensual tactile experiences.

Create mood boards that aesthetically please you.

Celebrate on Fridays and let yourself play, whether in company or by yourself. Friday is for fun.

Romance yourself – make loving yourself the best relationship you'll ever have.

FEELING UNBALANCED?

Work through emotional debris with a good therapist or counsellor.

Enjoy an injection of inspirational art.

Adorn your living space with the scents that most resonate.

Indulge in some luscious chocolates, fruits, sweet teas, cake, delicious poetry, or canoodling in front of a heartwarming film.

VENUS
MEDITATION

FOR SELF-LOVE

✦
|
|
|
|
|
|
|
✦

This simple meditation is designed to enhance your feelings of self-love in minutes. It is perfect for when you're feeling a bit down on yourself or if you want to work on enhancing self-worth. You can do this exercise anytime, anywhere, but it is truly Venusian to do it in bed, in a scented bath (don't fall asleep!) or even while gazing in the mirror at your gorgeous face.

Sit or lie down in a comfortable,
quiet spot where you won't be disturbed.

Put your hands over your heart and imagine yourself
surrounded by a comforting cloud of pink light that radiates from
your heart centre.

Take six deep, long breaths, slowly and gently, in and
out, without straining. Imagine yourself breathing in all the love
and breathing out all the non-loving thoughts and feelings.

Repeat the following affirmation as many times as feels right for
you (six is great, but don't worry if you lose count). You can say the
words out loud or in your mind – whatever works for you, and that
can change on any given day.

I am love.
I am lovable.
I love myself.

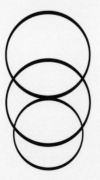

NEPTUNE

CONDUIT ✦ **PROPHET** ✦ *DREAMER*

THE NUMBER 7

✦✦✦

The number 7 has been considered mystical since the ancient peoples first discerned seven visible celestial bodies in the night sky. In the Bible, God took six days to make the Earth and rested on the seventh day, which is where the belief that the number 7 symbolises God arose – the seventh day was God's day. There are seven deadly sins and seven layers of hell, which don't sound promising. Neither does seven years of bad luck, which, according to superstition, is what you get after breaking a mirror. In Judaism, there are the seven lamps, or candles, of the golden menorah, which are associated with the seven ancient visible planets (the Sun and Moon included).

On a non-spiritual level, 7 is also a highly significant number. We have seven days of the week, and four seven-day lunar phases make up the Moon cycle. The visible light spectrum has seven colours, the rainbow comprises these seven colours, there are seven notes in most musical scales, and we have even chosen seven wonders of the world. Very many people consider 7 to be their special and lucky number; I've lost count of the times I've asked someone their favourite number and the answer is 7. The heptagon is the geometric shape of the number 7, while the seven-pointed heptagram or septagram star is thought to possess magical powers to repel evil.

In numerology, 7 represents spirituality, going within, the mysteries of life and transcending the material world. The number 7 governs our perception, containing possibilities such as insight, foresight and the clarity that comes from deeper truths, as well as delusion, illusion and the imperceptible. It also rules our extra-sensory perceptions, such as psychic awareness and the ability to know what is not always plainly showing. The dream world, the astral plane, the subconscious, unconscious and superconscious mind are all in 7's domain.

NEPTUNE

✦✦✦

Named for the Roman god of water and the oceans, Neptune is symbolised by the trident. Neptune's three-pronged trident is said to represent the three bodies of water – the seas, rivers and streams – and the three physical attributes of water – liquidity, fecundity and drinkability. It also represents matter, with its lower cross and the three curved prongs thought to embody the divine trinity of body, mind and spirit. Neptune teaches us about overcoming matter to reach higher dimensions. There is a heightened sensitivity that comes with this planet, as well as emotional depth and a yearning to know the unknowable.

Neptune is a most mysterious and remote planet. It was discovered in 1846 by a collective effort from two astronomers and a mathematician, although Galileo observed it first (he thought it was a star). Neptune is an ice giant – four times wider than Earth and a dark, cold, extremely windy place. It is the furthest planet from the Sun in our solar system and boasts a collection of fourteen moons and five hazy rings. It is very much like the other 'unseen' planet, Uranus, in composition, with a similar light blue colouring. Neptune rotates quickly (a Neptunian day lasts around sixteen hours) and orbits slowly, taking around 165 years to circle the Sun.

Neptune rules the numinous, the nebulous and the unseen. Dreams, the subconscious and unconscious (both individual and collective), moods and the wounds and projections of our psyches are all under Neptune's spell. Neptune resonates with the energies of the otherworld, the underworld and the metaphysical. Neptunian artistry, whimsy and fantasy create beautiful magic in our lives. When these aspects spill over into escapism and addiction, though, they can become powerful dark forces. Spiritual evolution is the goal of Neptune. Removing illusion and delusion is its lesson.

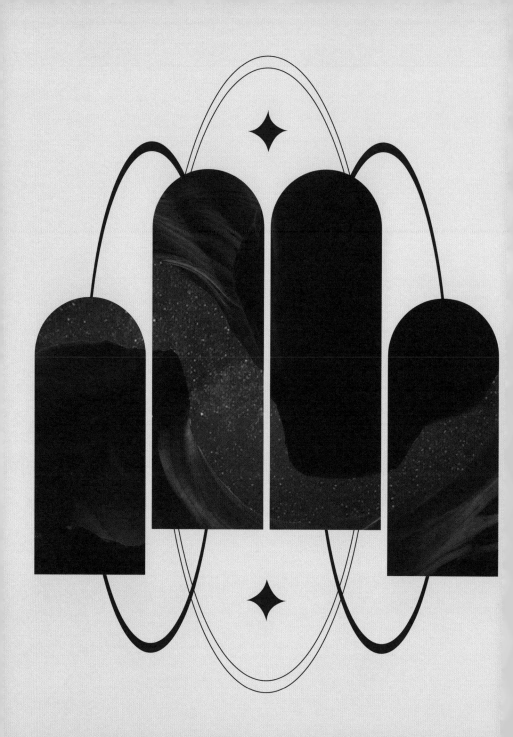

7

✦

NEPTUNE FOUNDATION

✦————————————————————✦

*NEPTUNE DOES NOT HAVE
A FOUNDATION PLACEMENT,
AS THERE IS NO DAY
OF THE WEEK NAMED
AFTER NEPTUNE*

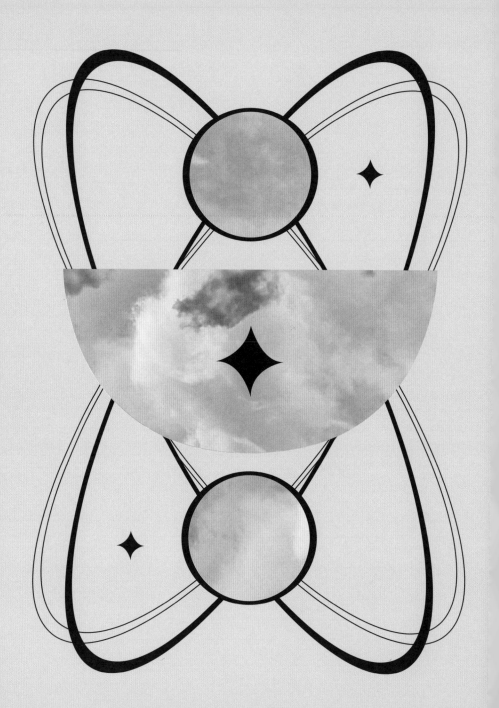

7

✦

NEPTUNE PERSONALITY

✦────────────────────────────✦

DAY
OF THE
MONTH
YOU
WERE
BORN

=

7

7

NEP
TU
NE

PERSONALITY ● DAY OF THE MONTH YOU WERE BORN = 7

Neptune personalities have a delightfully nebulous and ethereal energy about them. There is a certain mystery to this personality placement and you are likely to be drawn to the mystical side of life. Your character is more introspective, contemplative and quiet, emanating a gentleness. There is always heightened sensitivity with Neptunes and you are very much an empath, which can make you emotionally vulnerable and easily hurt or disturbed by other people. Your boundaries can be gossamer thin – this is something to work on reinforcing, so that you aren't upset by people's thoughtlessness.

The Neptune energy is languid and soft but, make no mistake, there is great power within you. Being a deep feeler and highly emotional human gives you a lot of insight into inner worlds and a beautiful ability to understand what other people go through in life. You are definitely someone others can turn to when they need a compassionate listener. You not only feel the full spectrum, but you are also able to pick up on and sense the energies of places, situations and people. You have the ability to tune in to the unseen and unspoken; this is a superpower that you can train to help you, by showing you where the good stuff is and keeping you out of trouble.

There is a changeable quality to your personality. Some might say moody, but it's really just that you can shift with the wind and are adaptable (sometimes even reactive) to your surroundings. Because of your sensitive and receptive nature, it is important that you connect with and surround yourself with good eggs. The people in your surroundings, and the surroundings themselves, affect you deeply – make sure they are nurturing you. Do not allow emotionally unsafe people to enter your life. If they sneak in, boot them out immediately and mercilessly. You are a gentle soul and must protect yourself.

Neptune people are the conduits of the world, able to pull the most beautiful inspirations seemingly from thin air. You are a poet and your creative capacity is huge, even if you don't realise it. Neptunes are the dreamers and from their

222

magical, conceptual minds they can bring whole new worlds into existence. You can easily become lost in a reverie and might find it hard to stay focused and grounded. With Neptune in this placement you have an impressive level of wisdom and imagination – you are a true original. You're all about the *layers* of the message, rather than screaming the message from the rooftops. Although the squeaky wheels can often grab the initial attention, they lack your substance and ability to truly capture an audience. Use your depth and make it work for you.

The Neptune personality is often a bit of an escape artist, because emotional pain can be so unbearable that they want to avoid it at all costs. This can manifest in many ways, from the obvious substance addictions to some of the less obvious ones, such as shopping, food, romance and sex. There is a part of Neptune that loves a good heady thrill, but where this gets dangerous for you is when it's done to evade your inner truths. Face up to your difficulties and struggles and seek as much healing support as you need, for as long as you need, rather than go down the road of self-destruction.

Sorcery, magic, the spiritual, sacred and arcane are all under the rule of Neptune and many of you will have this type of interest. It might take the form of religious devotion or be way out in the hippie zone. Either way, with Neptune in this placement, this aspect of your life is highly important and it's beneficial for you to connect with what you believe. Having a relationship with the divine nourishes your soul and provides a strength that can't be found elsewhere. Whether it's a church or a coven of witches, you need a thriving spiritual life to support you. Neptune personalities crave grounding and stability. Creating healthy routines and maintaining solid foundations will give you the infrastructure to keep yourself in balance. Strengthen your self-discipline and keep your basic life structures and routines strong.

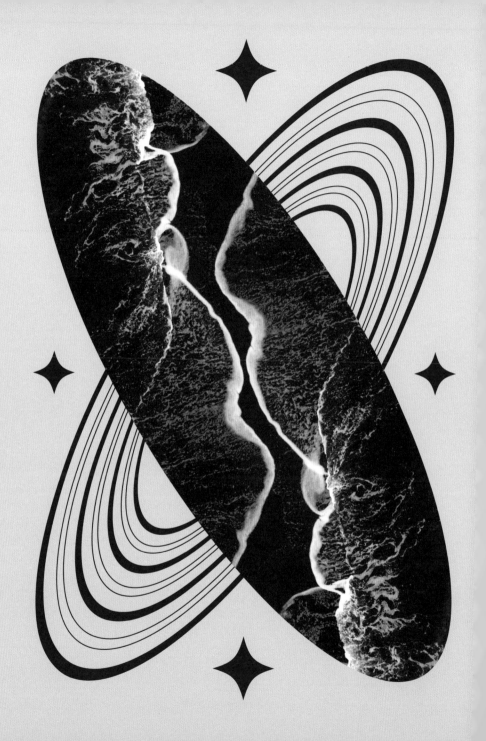

7

✦

NEPTUNE DESTINY

✦ ————————————————————————— ✦

DAY

+

MONTH

+

YEAR

=

7

Neptune destinies love the obscure and unusual and are definitely not your average Joes. There are so many worlds upon worlds that you will explore in your lifetime, and the journeys you are most interested in are of the inner kind. There is a profound wisdom to most Neptunes, which comes from their general tendency to be contemplative. Neptunes want to know and understand, and it's not the facts and figures type of knowledge that they're after. The Neptune destiny loves to explore the meaning of life and ensure that life is full of meaning. It's way too dull and boring to just go through the motions and skim the surface. You like to go deep.

Neptune loves mystery and bringing things to light. Your spirituality will grow as you grow, and you will often study widely on esoteric, philosophical or religious subjects. There is a prophet-like energy to the Neptune destiny – you really do think and feel deeply. You might not talk much, because you don't see the point in saying something unless it's meaningful. Many a Neptune destiny gets the 'could apply themself more' comment on their school report because of a tendency to daydream. There is nothing wrong with having an active imagination – it's how you use it that counts and, as an adult, creative thinking skills are a huge asset.

Creativity is Neptune's middle name and your skill in combining intuition, emotion and intellect is second to none. Your ideas are well rounded when you stay grounded in reality, and you can bring amazing inspirations into being when you work on your discipline. The occult and underworld are also the domain of Neptune and uncovering mysteries of life speaks to your philosophical nature. You have the ability to see what most others can't see as easily, and you can operate in both the seen and unseen worlds. This is an incredible gift – you can pick up on energies and read what is hidden between the lines.

With all these special skills, there are several areas of interest that can very much suit you career-wise. Therapy is an obvious one, and the somatic and psychotherapeutic disciplines speak to your talents. Neptune loves to look at and heal the subconscious and awaken higher levels of consciousness. Kinesiology, reiki, bodywork and other energy-informed practices would suit, as would any form of natural medicine. Working with water is another area that fits Neptune destinies. Many Neptunes use their intuition professionally, as readers, mediums or in the psychic realm, too. Probing the deeper mysteries of mathematics, science, behaviour, society, mythology, history and religion is also very Neptunian.

Neptune loves to look at and heal the subconscious and awaken higher levels of consciousness.

7

✦

NEPTUNE RELATIONSHIPS

✦ ─────────────── ✦

YOUR
DESTINY
NUMBER

+

THEIR
DESTINY
NUMBER

=

7

Dreamy, soft and gentle are beautiful characteristics of Neptune connections. This relationship can be a true source of comfort, provided you don't project too much of your own baggage onto each other. You are offered the opportunity to know the other person deeply when Neptune governs your connection. Subconscious issues will definitely come up for resolution. This relationship can play out old stories or press on old wounds, but it is an opportunity for unity, peace and healing. Handled well and with maturity, whatever shows its face in this relationship can change you both for the better. Have empathy and view the other with compassion.

Even if it's not obvious that this is a highly emotionally charged relationship, there's no escaping that fact. This can be a great thing, though, provided you ensure it's an emotionally nurturing and safe space for both of you. Neptune produces amazingly creative pairings, and you can make great things together. This is a deep, intuitive connection and you can divine and absorb the other person's energy with almost no barrier between you – but be careful with that. Make sure you maintain your own sovereignty.

In Neptune love relationships, falling head over heels is a common occurrence. That first flush of love, when you are completely deluded about the perfection of the other person, is so Neptune that it hurts. A little head-in-the-clouds love is a great rush, but you don't want to overindulge. Nothing beats loving a whole person and being loved for the whole of who you are. This relationship has much healing potential and you can enjoy sweetness and tenderness together. Don't run when it gets tricky, but navigate your way around difficult patches (within reason, of course – if abuse is happening, that's never a 'difficult patch' and you should leave immediately). Neptune relationships can have a compulsive element; don't head down the road of co-dependency. Avoid self-sabotage and don't let subconscious fears and projections taint the relationship. Keep your connection clean with honesty, compassion and steadfastness.

KINDRED NEPTUNE ASSOCIATES

These are the special friends of Neptune, connected and aligned with the whimsical energy of this mystical and ethereal planet. They embody Neptunian characteristics and can be called upon to support or enhance your Neptune energy, whether or not this is one of your planets. Use this information and work with Neptune to balance, inspire, heal and make magic happen.

7

NEP
TU
NE

KINDRED ASSOCIATES

POWER COLOURS

VIOLET AND BLUE-GREEN

Violet and pale blue–green are associated with Neptune. Violet is the
highest vibrating frequency of all the colours and is considered the most
spiritual, associated with higher thought and the higher self. The blue–
green hue of the ocean is also highly Neptunian.

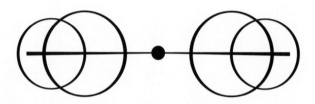

POWER DAY

THERE IS NO DAY OF THE WEEK NAMED
AFTER NEPTUNE

NEP
TU
NE

ASTROLOGICAL SIGN

PISICES

Neptune rules
the astrological
sign of Pisces,
although in
ancient astrology
Pisces was ruled
by Jupiter.

ELEMENT

WATER

Water is ruled by Neptune, but in a
metaphysical rather than physical way.
The spiritual, otherworldly and energetic
aspects of water – dreams, mystery,
intuition, feeling, empathy and the soul
or psyche – are all part of the watery
Neptune vibe.

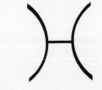

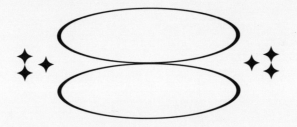

TAROT CARDS

The cards of the Chariot and the
Tower are numbered 7 and 16 in
the major arcana of the tarot, with
16 becoming 7 when you add 1 +
6. When you are working with or
learning about these cards, bring
your awareness to their Neptunian
characteristics – overcoming
whatever subconscious issues
might stand between you and
success, the removal of illusion and
realisation of truth, and moving
away from delusion to awakening.

BODY NURTURE ZONES

The thalamus – the part near the brain's centre that governs sleep, awareness and perception and delivers sensory messages – is the nurture zone for Neptune. The pineal gland is also ruled by Neptune, serving as the third eye and regulating circadian rhythms. Nourish the Neptunian nervous system and be aware of your mental, emotional and sensory diet. Sleep is vital.

ESSENTIAL OILS

Sandalwood

Jonquil

Champak

Rosewood

Aniseed

The Neptunian aromatics are calming and soothing, with a centring depth. They can be used in a diffuser or oil burner, as they're more ethereally attuned, or be diluted and applied topically. A little goes a long way with these aromas: they are quite potent and can be overwhelming.

SANDALWOOD is the quintessential meditation oil. It is super-balancing to calm those intense Neptune emotions, helping you stay clear and stable.

JONQUIL and CHAMPAK both have a heady, narcotic scent and otherworldly quality, but, at the same time, a groundedness that helps keep the dreamy Neptune vibe centred in the real world.

ROSEWOOD acts as a tonic for an overwhelmed nervous system, helping to ease the sense of fragility that can overcome sensitive Neptunes. ANISEED also has a tonic effect, reviving anyone who is burnt out or overstimulated.

HEALING HERBS

Mugwort

Passionflower

Aniseed

Lime blossom

Seaweed

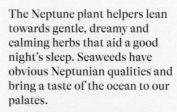

The Neptune plant helpers lean towards gentle, dreamy and calming herbs that aid a good night's sleep. Seaweeds have obvious Neptunian qualities and bring a taste of the ocean to our palates.

MUGWORT is well known as a dream enhancer and is used traditionally as a tonic for its calming, yet strengthening, properties.

PASSIONFLOWER is a sedative, perfect for assisting with sleep.

ANISEED is a fragrant, warming, delicate, yet potent, herb with a fortifying energy. It is used to help with sleep and digestive issues.

LIME BLOSSOM (linden) is a gently sedating classic bedtime herb with a sweet, nurturing energy.

Adding a little SEAWEED to your diet is great to naturally boost iodine levels and help you tune in to Neptune's oceanic energy. Iodine levels are high in seaweed, so just a sprinkle is plenty – and talk to your doctor first if you have thyroid issues.

KINDRED ASSOCIATES

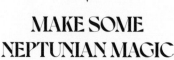

MAKE SOME NEPTUNIAN MAGIC

Meditate, accompanied by music and scent, to capture your imagination.

Practise with the tarot, oracle cards, a dowsing pendulum, runes or the *I Ching*. Divination is very Neptune.

Make an appointment with a reputable psychic, medium or intuitive reader.

Get in touch with the Earth by taking a nature walk.

FEELING UNBALANCED?

Water heals Neptune. Bathe, swim or go for a walk in the rain to cleanse your aura.

Massage can work wonders for a Neptune who is feeling disconnected from the self.

Sometimes a good cry helps to release stuck emotion and stress.

See an energy healer and get recalibrated.

NEEDING INSPIRATION?

Wear the colour violet or pale blue–green, or add these colours to your home zone.

Have your astrological or numerological chart drawn up to learn more about yourself.

Go on a spiritual retreat or take a day of silent, no-technology contemplation at home alone.

Keep a dream diary and marvel at the wisdom of your subconscious as you tune in to the symbology and what it means to you.

NEPTUNE MEDITATION

FOR STRENGTHENING INTUITION

Have you ever had a moment when you just *knew* something or someone was or wasn't right? You might not have listened, but it turned out your gut instinct was spot on? That's intuition and we all have it. Your perception is no less capable than anyone else's. It's like a muscle: the more you work it, the stronger it becomes. Everyone receives information from their higher self all the time – the trick is to take notice of the subtle energies you're picking up on.

The more you listen, the more noticeable and frequent these intuitive nudges become. They act almost like a reward system. However, it's important to be aware that the head can get in the way of your knowing, or even masquerade as intuitive intelligence. Your intuition will never sound like your inner critic; it's always a more loving energy, even when it's telling you things you don't want to hear. So always ask, 'Is this coming from love, and for my ultimate highest good?' before you act. If you aren't sure, do nothing and wait until you are.

This meditation is designed to help train your inner knowing muscle so your guidance system grows stronger.

Grab paper and something to write with.

Sit or lie down in a quiet, comfortable place where you won't be
disturbed or distracted.

Think of a question you have about something in your
life right now and ask your higher self this question. You can ask
it out loud, write it down or say it internally. It's best to start with
smaller questions when you are beginning, things that aren't overly
emotionally charged for you.

Sit quietly and breathe gently, slowly and deeply
until the information starts to flow in.
Be patient and listen to the quiet voice.

Whatever comes to mind, ask yourself,
is this your truth or a projection?

Write down whichever bits of intelligence
gold pass that inner truth test.

Now you can wait and see how it pans out. You won't always be
right, but you will start to differentiate between true and false
guidance. You can also use divination or oracle cards with this
exercise – ask your question and then write down the first things
that come through when you look at the cards you have drawn.

SATURN

TIMELESS ✦ **DISCIPLINED** ✦ *HEALER*

THE NUMBER 8

✦✦✦

The number 8 represents eternity. It speaks of that which is endless, limitless, immortal, timeless and infinite. The cycle of birth, life, death and rebirth, or the afterlife (depending on your belief system), is inherent in the design of the number. The mathematic glyph for infinity is represented by an 8 on its side: ∞. An infinite cycle of energy, the theory that energy can never be destroyed or lost, only transformed into a different type of energy, is one of the scientific laws of thermodynamics. These laws intersect science, religion and the metaphysical, and resonate with the energy of 8.

The number 8 is attuned to wealth, money and success. Determination, longevity, and building strong structures with stable foundations are all concepts attributed to 8. A number of great power requires discipline to make the best use of that power, and 8 is only going to work for you if you work for it. There's no such thing as a free lunch around here. If 8 were a person, they would be someone whose trust and respect you'd need to earn. Once you've managed that, you will have a loyal friend for life. The rewards promised by 8 are immense but not easily gained. They are worth the effort, though.

In Chinese culture, 8 is considered lucky because it sounds like the word that means 'to prosper'. In Hinduism, 8 also means wealth and prosperity. In Paganism, there are eight Sabbats celebrated – the special festivals that mark turning points in the wheel of the year. The Sabbats include the winter and summer solstices and the spring and autumn equinoxes. The most famous of the Sabbats is, of course, the Celtic Samhain, also now known as Halloween. The noble eightfold path of Buddhism consists of eight practices, taught by the Buddha and outlining the route to liberation, enlightenment and the end of suffering. In yogic philosophy, we see a similar teaching from Patanjali, known as the eight limbs of yoga.

SATURN

aturn is another of the gorgeous gas giants, like Jupiter. It is adorned with a spectacular series of seven major rings, made up of thousands of icy ringlets that sparkle in the sky. Saturn has a gang of many moons and moves slowly across the sky. It is about nine times wider than Earth and is the sixth furthest planet from the Sun. Saturn is named for the Roman god Saturnus, who ruled the domains of wealth, the seasons, time and agriculture. Saturnus was known for his wise leadership and for providing the foundations of prosperity to farmers.

Saturn is most famously known as the ruler of time. This applies to personal lifetimes, families across generations, eternity and infinity. Healing is another great gift from this planet, with Saturn also ruling karma and karmic inheritance. Limitation is a Saturnine characteristic, as is discipline, and we should remember that these qualities are actually good for us. Without the tempering influence of Saturn, we would be spoilt rotten. The influence of time can be beneficial, too. If everything came to us instantly, at our merest whim, we would value none of it. When we have to wait, we appreciate. These karmic concepts teach us to stay on the path of goodness; discipline is something every person needs to be effective.

All the talent in the world comes to naught if we can't direct, hone and refine it. The gifts that Saturn bestows might not have been at the top of our wish list, but they are very useful. A strong work ethic and the commitment to see things through are so Saturnine. Judgement is another aspect of human nature and society that is governed by Saturn. It's fashionable to talk about 'non-judgement' in spiritual circles, but if we lack discernment (the positive version of judgement) we are likely to make terrible choices. And that's something Saturn would absolutely hate to see us do.

8

• SATURN

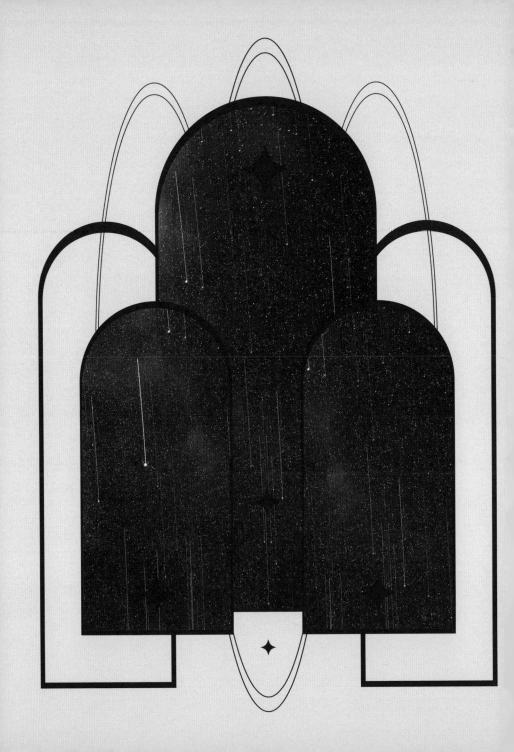

8

✦

SATURN
FOUNDATION

⟡————————————⟡

DAY
OF THE
WEEK
YOU
WERE
BORN

=

SATURDAY

Saturday-born people are the strongest and most solid personalities of all. Truthful and true to themselves, what you see is absolutely what you get. Honesty is always the best policy when you are a Saturn, or are dealing with one.

With this planet as your foundation, you cannot stand inauthenticity, in yourself or anyone else. Saturn foundations like to face reality and accept it for what it is but, if they don't like that reality, they will either work hard to change it or walk away entirely. You have to live a genuine life and can't understand how anyone else can do otherwise. Fairness and being genuine are at the core of who you are.

It would be remiss not to point out that Saturns often face more life challenges than most, and adversity creates astuteness and wisdom. The role of the wise elder, with an awareness that others don't possess, is Saturn personified. This foundation placement gives you the maturity, resilience and life skills that make it possible for you to overcome any obstacle and make something good of it. Forgive other people for being less able to live authentically, or have as much of a moral compass. When something really matters, worry about that, but otherwise a bit of 'live and let live' will help to greatly reduce your stress levels. Wallowing in negativity, reminiscing or criticising is natural in small doses, but in excess it becomes a darkness trap. Learn to let go. Life is for living, and all we have is now.

Once you are able to embrace your pain, acknowledge everything you've been through and choose to use it to fuel your rise, then you will embrace your power. Saturn foundations can accumulate a lot of success, accomplishments and wealth. People with this foundation planet are the quiet achievers, who work hard and slowly build their dream life brick by brick. You know that if you want something, no amount of wishful thinking will create it: you have to put in the effort. You are loyal, steadfast and take on a lot, sometimes assuming too much responsibility for others and situations that aren't your crosses to bear. Saturns are protective of those under their wing and give tough love. Saturn whips those in their inner circle into shape. What drives that is the deepest caring.

Saturns can become cynical and overtired of other people's issues and the ways of the world. When this happens, spring yourself out of the world-weary trap and tap into the people, things and activities that bring you joy. Let go of yearning for the past, or holding on to it too tightly. Sometimes Saturns get so tied up in work, obligations and an overarching sense of generalised responsibility that they forget they're a person, too. You have needs, just like everyone else. You deserve good times, days off and a little lightness. Don't be too restrictive with yourself. Allow some treats, allow some pampering and let yourself have a little luxury here and there. It's the simple things that bring you the most happiness, so allow yourself to have them, plus the odd extra frivolous treat. You really do deserve it.

To bring out the best in this foundation placement, find the things in life that truly ring your bell and dedicate yourself to them. Because you are diligent, conscientious and such a hard worker, you bring success to any endeavour that speaks to your heart. Work on being comfortable with who you are, have pride in the strength of your character and value your authenticity. Don't bother buying into the superficiality all around you; put your attention on what matters most to you and ignore what society says. You are the real deal: embrace that. No apologies. Consult your inner wisdom – for you have plenty – and trust in your own intelligence. Practise kindness towards yourself first and then radiate it outwards. Whenever you find yourself feeling harsh about yourself, or something external, go gently. Saturns need softness and lightness, too.

8

✦

SATURN PERSONALITY

✦——————————————————✦

DAY
OF THE
MONTH
**YOU
WERE
BORN**
=
8

The Saturn personality type has a great deal of awareness. Naturally conscious, you are awake and attentive to all aspects of the people and the world around you, as well as within yourself. Naturally rich in love, you care a lot and have a strong social conscience. You are aware that everything you do and say in this life has an impact, and you do your best to make that impact a good one. You want to add to the world, not take from it, and you have a lot to give. Saturn personalities love fiercely and your love isn't just confined to other people. Many a Saturn is a huge nature- and animal-lover, and they are often the people out there supporting worthy causes in any way they can. Saturn can make you a bit of a traditionalist who loves rituals and customs.

Determination is your middle name. Once you commit to something, you're all in. You hate to give up or walk away from anyone or anything you have invested time or energy in. This can obviously be a double-edged sword and something to be aware of as a potential life trap. It's okay to cut your losses when it really is a hopeless case or has caused you too much suffering. Studious and meticulous, the Saturn personality pays attention to detail, does things properly the first time round and would rather do nothing than do it by half. This is a valuable trait, especially in the workplace. Make sure that you are rewarded and acknowledged correctly for the level of effort you bring. Don't end up carrying everyone else who can't be bothered to achieve competence. Modesty is another attribute common to Saturns. While it's a great thing not to be overly attention seeking, it does serve you to know your worth and expect to be treated accordingly.

The early life of the Saturn personality is often difficult and it's important, if that's you, to know that life truly can become better. Most Saturn personalities have lives that improve with age. They are often the seemingly late bloomers, who grow successful and enjoy greater wellbeing after their youth. Try not to lose faith for long. No matter what happens, never give up on love and never give up hope in life's ability to transform. Saturn takes time to bring things around. Be patient and keep to your path. Family, lineage, legacy and ancestral issues are the obstacle course a Saturn personality must navigate before they can fully bloom. You are likely to be the one that breaks the mould of your family pattern and, in so doing, you bring great healing to your bloodline.

People with this personality placement are very intolerant of phoneys. You love to help those who are in difficulty and your honest and charitable nature is a beautiful thing. Serene when in alignment, you owe it to yourself and everyone around you to look after *you* and maintain all the things that bring you balance and relieve you of stress. Saturns can be risk averse, although once they have trust in themselves this can change and life can become a beautiful adventure. Everything opens up to you when they let themselves relax and experience ease. It's common with Saturn in this placement to push yourself and demand very high levels of excellence at all times.

Saturn personalities also demand others be accountable and take responsibility. You expect them to commit and stay true to their word. It's unwise of anyone to lie to your face – you have a great built-in lie detector and you always know. People might fall short of your expectations – it's best to let that go most of the time. Although it can be hard to forget when someone has let you down, unless it's a sackable offence, try to move on. Saturn personalities really like to do their own thing, but can be controlling of other people. Allow them the same amount of rope you would give yourself. You absolutely can take on a lot and achieve much over the course of your lifetime. Saturns like to reach, to challenge themselves and to always become better. With this attitude, you are sure to progress, accomplish much and evolve greatly in life.

8

✦

SATURN
DESTINY

DAY

+

MONTH

+

YEAR

=

8

The Saturn destiny placement lends you a certain gravitas as a person. Saturn gives you the blessing of personal power, discipline, simplicity and integrity. People know what they are getting with you and you possess a depth and grace that is intimidating to the wrong people and hugely attractive to the right ones. You have both style and substance, a rare combination indeed. When Saturn is your destiny planet, you have the capacity to endure and succeed at whatever you put your mind and will to. Often those with a Saturn destiny find their calling a little later in life, building on accomplishment after accomplishment until they find their happy place in the world. The so-called 'overnight sensation', who actually took ten years of working hard to make it, is a classic Saturn destiny story.

You are tenacious, and you take responsibility on both a personal and external level in your life. Be careful not to shoulder other people's burdens, though: you can be a bit too willing to wear the price that isn't yours to pay. Beware the saviour complex. Yes to taking care of yourself and the people in your life as appropriate; no to carrying another's weight for them. It will only make you angry at the world. Use that brilliant work ethic for your own benefit, too.

All Saturns have a deep spirituality. For this placement, in particular, your connection to your faith will grow throughout your life. It is also likely that your faith will be tested and come out stronger than anything life can throw at it. Your beliefs are your bedrock.

When it comes to your talents and how Saturn can work for you in the career spectrum, you have an affinity for anything to do with good causes, charity and social-related areas, or other fields that make a difference to the greater good. Saturn rules wealth, so the financial, investment and business sector is a boon for you (your sensibility truly pays dividends). History, teaching and education are obvious gifts for the wise Saturn. Agriculture is an area traditionally associated with Saturn – this might seem odd until you realise how connected to patience and the process of time this area is. Freedom and justice are natural Saturn environments, so anything to do with the law suits your innate sense of right and wrong. The healing arts, as well as spiritual practices and religion, are very Saturnine and you bring a much-needed down-to-earth energy to this kind of work.

Often those with a Saturn destiny find their calling a little later in life, building on accomplishment after accomplishment until they find their happy place in the world.

8

✦

SATURN RELATIONSHIPS

*YOUR
DESTINY
NUMBER*
+
**THEIR
DESTINY
NUMBER**
=
8

The Saturn relationship is a healing relationship. This can sometimes be a challenging connection to maintain, as it forces you to face up to aspects of yourself that are difficult to confront. Remember, this is a very beautiful and precious thing: echo chambers are dangerous places to inhabit. With every difficulty the two of you have to manage, you are both delivered a golden opportunity to mature as people, heal your wounds and ultimately be free. Saturn doesn't shy away from reality and hide in the comfort of fantasy and delusion. Instead, this planet shines a harsh light of truth on whatever needs to be restored, repaired, renewed or removed in order for you to operate as your higher self. Easy? No. Worth it? Yes. A thousand times over.

This relationship demands equality. The right amount of give and take creates an atmosphere where both of you can thrive. Balancing the level of closeness and space is another area this connection demands you pay attention to. There is no over-enmeshment or suffocation allowed. Healthy boundaries are a must. Saturn is the ultimate teacher and, whatever type of relationship this is, you will grow as people from knowing each other. You will learn how to be better versions of yourselves. Avoid criticism, let go of controlling tendencies, communicate gently, share feedback in a loving way with a positive spin, and the trust in this bond can be unbreakable. Saturn relationships can truly give you the best, truest, strongest and most faithful friend you've ever had. Do right by each other, practise patience and acceptance and you can be each other's rocks for life.

When it comes to the romantic version of the Saturn alliance, you are both required to step up, show up and grow up. You must be willing to be both teacher and pupil with this one. Relationships take work – on yourselves, on each other and on the relationship – if you want them to last. That's just reality, and all the hearts and flowers in the world won't make up for shaky foundations and zero effort. The beauty of the Saturn love relationship is its immense potential for lifelong devotion and the kind of love that grows stronger and more beautiful over the years. All this and more can be yours if you are both willing to make the effort. Avoid harshness in your interactions, and consider the other with unconditional positive regard and 100 per cent respect. Think of yourselves as gentle guides for each other's unfolding greatness.

Saturn is the ultimate teacher and, whatever type of relationship this is, you will grow as people from knowing each other.

KINDRED
SATURN
ASSOCIATES

These are the special friends and correspondences of Saturn, connected and aligned with the strength, wisdom and powerful energy of this noble planet. They embody Saturn characteristics and can be called upon to support or enhance your Saturnine energy, whether or not this is one of your planets. Use this information and work with Saturn to balance, inspire, heal and make magic happen.

BLACK AND PURPLE

Black is so Saturn. It is the most practical, classic and elegant colour of all, with a dash of mature sexiness thrown in for good measure. Deep purple is also associated with Saturn, as it represents wisdom, tradition, spirituality, lineage, wealth and royalty.

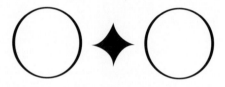

SATURDAY

For people with Saturn placements, every Saturday is extra special and supportive. Even if you don't have Saturn as one of your planets, you can connect with these properties for a more aligned day. Saturday is the day for discipline. Sounds boring, I know, but if your housework, health needs, life admin and family obligations are not dealt with, they pile up, overwhelm and drag you down. Nobody needs that burden hanging over their head. Saturn is all about foundational elements, such as money, home, schedules, family and energy management. Balance these and everything else falls into place. Saturn is beautifully pragmatic: just don't fall into the comfortable trap of being a negatron that looks only for fault or what could go wrong. Look for the good to keep your mood up. Saturday is a perfect day to get practical and sort out life.

ASTROLOGICAL SIGN

CAPRICORN

ELEMENT

EARTH

The element associated with Saturn is earth. Like Saturn, earth has a robust denseness, which brings feelings of stability, solidity and strength. The earth element is grounding and speaks to practical matters.

TAROT CARDS

The cards of Strength and the Star are numbered 8 and 17 in the major arcana of the tarot, with 17 becoming 8 when you add 1 + 7. When studying the tarot cards or performing readings, you will now know these cards are associated with the energies of the number 8 and Saturn. Their themes of fortitude, patience, balance, wisdom gained from discipline, hopefulness, having courage and faith against all odds, overcoming obstacles, criticism and pessimism, the healing of old wounds, and divine timing are all truly Saturnine.

BODY NURTURE ZONES

Saturn governs our bones, joints, teeth and mineral balance, as well as the spleen and gallbladder, those supposedly non-major organs that are actually very important. When Saturn is one of your planets, it is important to prevent stiffening of your structure by moving, maintaining suppleness, alignment and good posture, and nourishing your bones. Keep an eye on your mineral levels.

ESSENTIAL OILS

Pine

Cypress

Cedarwood atlas

Myrrh

Patchouli

The Saturnine essential oils are fortifying, grounding and powerfully aromatic. Several are derived from ancient trees. They can be used in diffusers or burners, or diluted and applied topically to relieve tension and pain.

PINE and CYPRESS are timeless evergreen ancients. These fresh, uplifting oils are excellent pain relievers and help with inflammation and stiffness, and bone and joint issues.

CEDARWOOD ATLAS is deeply grounding with a comforting sweetness. It provides strength to the spirit in trying times.

MYRRH is derived from a hard resin and connected to the otherworld. One of the oldest and most precious aromatics, it facilitates healing.

PATCHOULI facilitates spiritual connection, keeping the deep and introverted Saturn real and centred in their earthly physical body.

HEALING HERBS

Maritime pine

Horsetail

Valerian

Arnica

Comfrey

(Caution! Arnica and comfrey are for external use only and not on broken skin)

Saturn is all about structure; therefore, the Saturnine herbs are all about protecting, cleansing, reinforcing, renewing and strengthening the structures. They tend to be astringent and on the cold side energetically. The plants themselves tend to be hardy, just like Saturn people.

MARITIME PINE is rich in nutrients and an excellent antioxidant, traditionally used for immune and musculoskeletal support, wound healing and increasing bone strength.

HORSETAIL is famous as a nutritive herb for bone, skin and nail health.

VALERIAN is well known for reducing tension and stress and is a fantastic aid for deep restorative sleep.

ARNICA is reparative for bruised tissues and COMFREY is reparative for the joints and bones. These herbs are very powerful healers and are for external use only, not on broken skin.

SA
TU
RN

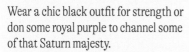

MAKE SOME SATURNINE MAGIC

Wear a chic black outfit for strength or don some royal purple to channel some of that Saturn majesty.

Get organised. Clutter in your surroundings is clutter in your mind, and Saturn loves a clean slate.

Celebrate and honour your ancestry through ritual, food or even just by lighting a candle.

Heal your body through practices and modalities that feel grounded and safe.

FEELING UNBALANCED?

Tune in to whatever higher power opens your heart and feeds your faith in life.

Saturn can grow a bit stagnant; moving your body facilitates the release of stuck energy.

Laughter is brilliant medicine for Saturn people. Comedy will help you lift a dull mood.

Find ways to share the benefits of your wisdom with other people.

NEEDING INSPIRATION?

Get out into nature. Nature soothes Saturn and removes stress, opening you up to a perspective refresh.

Learn about history, especially the history of your family or origin or cultural background.

Connect with the people you care about and engage in meaningful conversations.

Read the wisdom of those with an enlightened perspective and learn more about different philosophies and religions.

SATURN MEDITATION

FOR HEALING

✦
|
✦

This straightforward meditation focuses on healing whatever it is you would like to alleviate. This healing breathing practice can apply to specific areas of your life or yourself that you would like to let go of or improve. It can also be general, if you don't have a particular point of focus right now. The energy of Saturn lends itself perfectly to reduction; you can use this meditation to reduce the influence of negativity and welcome its opposite. Do this meditation whenever you feel the need, although before bed is ideal – it will work its magic while you sleep. All you require is intention and a pair of lungs. Healing doesn't have to be complicated: the simple things are often the most powerful.

Sit or lie down somewhere quiet and comfortable. Decide what it is you would like to work on and heal (this can be general and non-specific, such as 'stress', or very definitive, such as 'how I neglect my own needs to take care of others').

Then, find the counterpoint to your issue (so, in the above examples your counterpoint would be 'relaxation' and 'putting my needs first').

Breathe out slowly and steadily and let yourself feel empty.

Breathe in slowly, deeply and gently, without straining, imagining you are breathing in the solution to your problem.

As you breathe out slowly, deeply and gently, without straining, imagine you are releasing the problem and letting it go.

Focus on the breath and your intention to resolve and heal what needs healing.

Continue breathing in your solution and breathing out your problem until you feel it is time to finish.

Open your eyes and take a moment to let it all settle until you feel ready to get up again.

MARS

MAGNETIC ✦ **COURAGEOUS** ✦ *VICTORIOUS*

THE NUMBER 9

✦✦✦

Different cultures revere or fear the number 9. As the last single-digit number, it is considered the number of completion. In modern western numerology and astrology, there are nine celestial planets in addition to Earth (the Sun and Moon are included as 'planets'). There are also many examples in which 9 represents this completion: the 108 beads of the mala prayer beads, the 360 degrees of a complete circle and the nine months of a human pregnancy, to name just a few.

In Chinese culture, the number 9 is an auspicious number and is known as the number of heaven, while in Japan it is unlucky to say 9 because it sounds similar to the word for pain, torture or agony. Ancient Pythagorean numerologists believed 9 was an unlucky number because it falls one short of 10, which was seen as the number of perfection. Because 9 is considered a number of completion, it is also, by the same token, a number of beginnings and great potential. When the number 9 is multiplied by any other number, the result will always add up to 9. For example, $9 \times 5 = 45$, and $4 + 5 = 9$; or $9 \times 24 = 216$, and $2 + 1 + 6 = 9$; or $9 \times 5846 = 52,614 = 18 = 9$ ... However large the number, with fadic addition it becomes 9.

The number 9 has been through a lot to get to where it is; it has many associations with difficulties and battling suffering, and becoming tough and strong from that. There is plenty of power associated with 9, including physical, mental, magical and spiritual power. The number 9 also represents the humanitarians, crusaders and worthy-cause fighters of the world, who have become wise and seek to aid the downtrodden, the abused and the needy. Being of service, finding purpose and standing up for what's right is a very 9 approach to life.

MARS

✦✦✦

Mars is named for the Roman god of war, who creates bloodshed and whose symbols are the shield and spear. The Romans named the planet after Mars because its rusty red colour reminded them of blood. It is often referred to as the red planet and can be seen shining in the night sky like a large red star. The colour of this planet speaks of passion. Aggression, strength, confidence, power and energy are all associated with Mars, and this planet has a big presence, both physically and metaphysically.

Mars governs the dynamic, active principle and this relates to ambition, motivation, willpower, bravery, moving forwards, questing, competing and perseverance. Mars always finishes what it starts, preferably ahead of the field, too. Determination is a big Martian theme, as is setting a direction and heading into it. There are also aspects of the active principle that are challenging, such as recklessness, impulsiveness and being quick to fire up. The soil of Mars is rich in iron, as is human blood, which is where the many associations of Mars with the body and blood have gathered weight. Mars is considered the planet of surgery and represents our vital force (life blood), sex drive (creating bloodlines) and the circulation of blood around our body.

Although small in size, Mars is a solid and lively planet, complete with seasons, rugged and wild desert terrain, polar ice caps and changing weather. Although it is dry, dusty and cold now, astronomers have uncovered evidence that suggests Mars used to be much warmer, with active volcanoes and water. Martian terrain is now deep red, like rust, and is deemed currently inactive and supporting no life. Other than Earth, Mars is the most scientifically studied of all the planets, and the Mars 2020 Perseverance Mission by NASA recorded the first audio of the planet's sounds.

9

✦

MARS
FOUNDATION

◆━━━━━━━━━━━━━━━━━━◆

*DAY
OF THE
WEEK*
**YOU
WERE
BORN**

=

TUESDAY

9
MARS

The Mars foundation person is a red-hot package of charisma and sex appeal. A Martian exudes power, magnetism and vivacity. People feel your strength and significant atmosphere immediately when you enter a room. Energetic and arresting, willing, brave, determined and fierce, you aren't much afraid of anything, and if you do feel fear you never let it be seen. The courageous Mars does not shrink in times of crisis or need: you are always prepared for anything. Nothing surprises a Mars foundation – you were born ready.

With a strong constitution and lots of get up and go, the Mars foundation has a seemingly endless amount of stamina. Because of this, you can be prone to burnout from overtaxing your energy reserves. Be aware of that and take a rest before you think you need it. There is a natural exuberance to the Mars foundation – you are physically strong, often athletic, and radiate enthusiasm. Mars needs to physically move, exercise and maintain strength. If you are stressed, get moving, otherwise your energy goes inwards, becomes frustration, which becomes anger, and then ... look out everyone! Your body is very responsive and quick to heal, strengthen and get fit, too.

The Mars strength is both inner and outer. You have the courage to go for what you want in life and can focus your attention on what really matters to you. You are ambitious with a capital A and want to be at the top of your game. A Mars foundation takes action and moves quickly towards their goals. Being naturally expressive, you are not afraid to speak your truth or let people know how you think and feel. Honesty *is* your policy. You're all or nothing emotionally – the Mars foundation either cares very deeply, or not at all. It's nothing personal: you either love, dislike intensely or feel absolutely nothing.

Martians are super-loyal to their friends, family and partners. You will be there 100 per cent, without question, always. In romantic relationships, the Mars sexual prowess is legendary, but you generally aren't interested in anything frivolous. If you're not completely into it, you walk away and don't look back. Your inner circle might sometimes feel you're harsh or brutally abrupt, but they know they are fully loved and that you're honest with them. You don't have time or energy for lots of peripheral people, preferring to give your all to a chosen few.

Full of courage and personal power, you throw everything you've got at the stuff that matters to you. You need to be fully engaged in order to care about something. Why give anything if you're not going to give it all? You often become very successful through this determination and drive. You can tend towards 'bull in a china shop', so do read the room and temper your exuberance when it's the smart thing to do. Others can misunderstand the famous Mars intensity as being domineering, and be put off by it. You like to have your way and can seem pushy, because you're so very passionate.

Mars people are dynamic, driven, ambitious, active and bright, with lots of willpower. With Mars backing you up, you can accomplish pretty much anything if you're willing to work for it. It is important for the Mars person to find what they believe in and care about and direct their energy towards it. You can achieve a huge amount and be an incredible force for good when you dedicate yourself, so choose wisely where you put that power.

Anger and frustration are the Mars downfall. The energy of this planet is famously warlike; however, the flipside is peace. And Mars people do have the capacity to be very peaceful, believe it or not. The trick is to live in your integrity and not worry about how others are living, thinking, saying, doing, feeling. You can't control their behaviour or experience (and *you* hate to be controlled), so let things be. Reserve your fire for what matters. There is plenty in the world that needs fixing and you love to be proactive, so channel your fixer energy into things you can truly affect. Jealousy can get to you, too, especially if you feel the person doesn't deserve their luck.

You cannot abide cheats – those who do wrong and profit from it. Try not to focus on it too much; unless you can directly right the wrongs, it's not worth the stress. To bring out your best aspects, it's important you are an active force in your own life. You are meant to be a protagonist, forging ahead on your path. Maintain control over your destiny; it's vital that you do what is meaningful for you. By following your bliss, you are doing a service to yourself and the world. Frustration can't find you when you are living your truth. Maintain routines for a sense of stability and calm and make time to wind down and let go of your mission occasionally, so you can tune back in to you. Keep good people close, and forget about the rest.

9

✦

MARS
PERSONALITY

✦━━━━━━━━━━━━━━━━━━━━━━━✦

DAY
OF THE
MONTH
YOU
WERE
BORN

=

9

The Mars personality is bold, and anyone born on a 9, or number that adds to 9, is a true presence. Truly a force of nature, Martians are so powerful and strong that their aura can be felt before they enter the room. With Mars as your personality planet, you love victory and have the motivation and capacity to see things through. You rise to the challenge and are unrivalled in your capacity to give your all when you believe in something. You can be so hell bent on your mission that you forget all the other stuff, so do make time for everything else in your life. There is a competitive aspect to Mars, but you are never a bad sport; you keep things fair and will always fight for the underdog, if needed. Mars loves to back and defend the exploited and defenceless.

Mars personalities are tough, pragmatic and stoic, with loads of integrity. You'd never sit around whingeing and complaining; you take action and can't understand why others wouldn't. You are motivated to achieve by Mars, dogged and determined, and will push to finish, do your absolute best and aim high. With Mars in this placement, you are also appreciative, encouraging and motivating, especially to your friends, family and other loved ones. If someone is fortunate enough to have you onside, it's as if they have constant access to a brilliant life coach. Your approach is 'take no prisoners', so you won't mollycoddle anyone but will always try to help them do and be their best.

Mars makes you a fiery lover. Lucky is the person who ends up in your bed zone. You care passionately, and this level of care applies to lovers, friends, family and pretty much anyone else in your circle (you don't generally have people in that circle who you don't adore being around). You will do anything to help and support those close to you and are always willing to jump into the fray for someone you care about. Mars people make the best friends – loyal, expressive, loving and honest. Fawning just isn't in your skillset and fakery is anathema to your soul. You are a true friend, true love, true enemy – or nothing.

You are very kind, compassionate and honest with people. Watch out for your tendency for extreme honesty, though. Sometimes you can be a little bit too tough on people and they end up feeling you're like a boot-camp sergeant. Mars people do not like whiny types, or those who are always blaming someone else. People who constantly complain yet do nothing to resolve their situation make you crazy, as do lazy types. Avoid letting your annoyance flare with these people: it's better to let them be. If your frustration does erupt, although apologising isn't your forte, you will do well to say sorry occasionally to keep the social wheels turning. If you find yourself surrounded by boring whingers, find better friends.

Mars makes you adventurous, excitement loving, daring and brave. This can also make you a risk taker and a touch reckless at times, so do pause and take a breath before jumping. Famously impatient and impulsive, Mars needs to learn to slow down a bit and take it all in before making decisions. Then, once you've decided, you can act on your choices with full awareness. Give a Mars personality a job and they will carry it through: you never give up, slack off or drop the ball. The Mars prosecution lawyer is the defendant's worst nightmare. Mars doesn't do defeat. If you believe you are right, good luck to anyone who tries to change your mind. Also good luck to anyone who crosses you. Good luck and look out.

You won't stand for being overlooked, and you need to be around encouraging and appreciative people. If you lose trust in someone, it takes a lot for that trust to be restored. Once the damage is done, you will always be aware of that sore point. Maintain your sense of self-worth and surround yourself with people you can trust and who make you feel loved. If you become unmotivated or bogged down in pointless trivia, drama or tasks, you can become angry, stubborn and complacent. The lesson here is to dedicate yourself to the things you truly find fulfilling. No coasting allowed. You are capable and powerful – use your powers for good and you will always be satisfied.

285

9

✦

MARS
DESTINY

◆————————————————◆

DAY

+

MONTH

+

YEAR

=

9

Mars is the great manifestor and you can tune in to this vibe and create directly from the strength of your will and actions. Your life will likely resemble the classic hero's journey if you are a Mars destiny. You are the gladiators and Olympians of the human world and get where you need to be, even if it takes a long time and costs blood, sweat and tears. With Mars as your destiny planet, you are born to work hard for what you believe in, and to win. You have considerable willpower and won't quit unless it's truly called for. Mars is the heroic archetype – you smash through obstacles on your way to the next level of evolution in your life story.

You are a truly kind helper: Mars in your destiny placement gives you huge empathy levels and a willingness to serve humankind and the world we live in, and often the precious plants and animals, too. Ruled by your heart and conscience, and true to both, you are at your best crusading for your causes and giving your all to them from your huge reserves of love. A true friend and true believer, you stop at nothing to protect, assist and further those you love, what you feel is important and what you have faith in. When you want to help, you do everything in your power until you've succeeded. You are questing, striving, committed and supportive, and you see challenge as a beautiful gift. Your fighting Mars spirit is attuned to overcoming any hardship, struggle and limitation that gets in the way, and to growing into a better person from it.

Strong personalities with big energy, many a Mars destiny has been told they're 'too much'. This wound can lead to feeling shame, hiding your power and shrinking yourself, which is the opposite of your life mission. This trauma must be healed for you to be happy and comfortable with the magnificence of you. When you step into your power and have pride in your greatness, you are fully exalted and life will flow for you. It's not arrogant to know you have special gifts and talents and to be willing to use them as a force for splendour in the world.

You don't have to be bolshie to have self-respect and faith in yourself. Truly powerful people don't crow about it or throw their weight around. They just are.

In the vocation zone, Mars makes a great leader. You are able to infuse the whole team with energy, motivation and dedication to the greater cause. You will only follow if it is for the greater good and you can commit to it body, mind, heart and soul. You don't do red tape of any kind, so don't go for jobs that block creativity or crush your spirit with pointlessness. You need a free rein, so that you can take it all further than anyone else. Some areas suited to Mars are anything to do with the physical body and health, vocations that rely on strength or create it, such as engineering and building, and enforcing or fighting laws and rules. Justice, integrity, truth and fairness are all up the Mars alley, but this isn't always as obvious as being a judge. It's also very Martian to be an ecowarrior, social worker, advocate of human or animal rights, political campaigner, politician, journalist or ethicist.

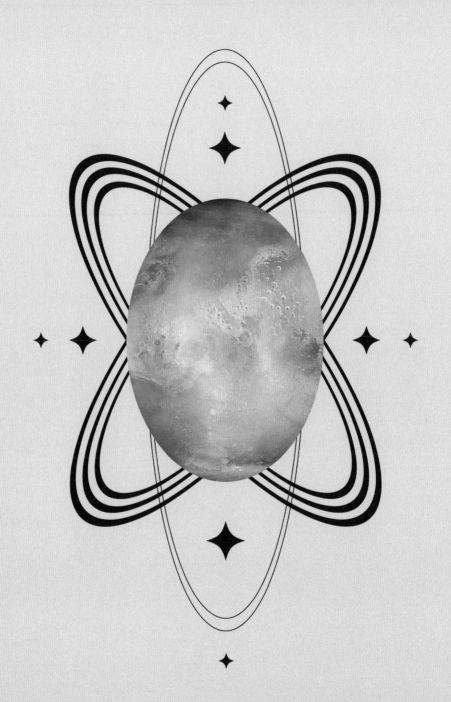

9

✦

MARS
RELATIONSHIPS

✦————————————————✦

YOUR
DESTINY
NUMBER
+

THEIR
DESTINY
NUMBER
=
9

Together, you can do anything. This connection is at its best when there's a shared cause, objective or goal that you can both direct your will and energy towards. The power of the two of you combined can move mountains. Freedom is necessary, and you must give each other the space to be who you are and not let small differences in values or opinions become huge bones of contention. Remember that in combination, you are great, and that wouldn't be the case if you were exactly the same. Watch out for an 'us and them' or an 'us against the world' combat mentality, too: it's not helpful in the long term.

You must stay united in the grand scheme of things, because disagreements can run deep. Direct the fight towards things you can both change for the better. Mars is the warrior and 'knight on a quest' archetype. Yes to making the world a better place; no to fighting against everything like a couple of misguided superheroes. Be ambitious together and work on passion projects; shared adventures bring this connection closer. Mars is the planet of action, and this is a less-talking, more-doing relationship. Serve this bond loyally and it can be the deepest of your life.

The song 'Light My Fire' was probably written with a Mars lover in mind. Passionate is the word that best describes the Mars love match, and on a scale of one to ten, the potential for a great sexual connection is an eleven. You will be fiercely protective of each other, always ready to back each other up. It can get intense between the two of you – sometimes too intense – so it's important to balance all that fiery heat with calming activities, times of peace and quiet, and plenty of willingness to compromise. Loyalty and honesty is everything.

Fighting and control issues can overtake the good in this relationship, so always be ready to apologise and admit when you are being unhelpful. This is a dynamic-duo power-couple vibe, and the two of you united can be a huge force in the world. Boredom is a passion killer, so keep it interesting.

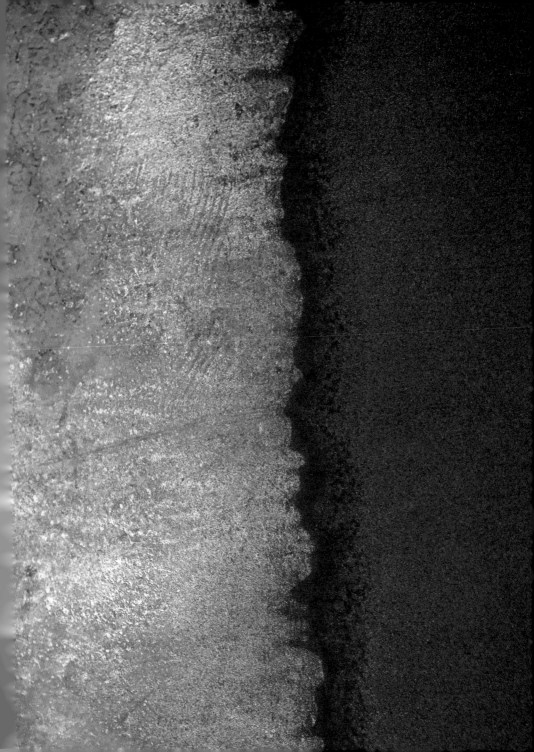

KINDRED
MARS
ASSOCIATES

These are the special friends of Mars, connected and aligned with the intense and active energy of this dynamic planet. They embody Martian characteristics and can be called upon to support or enhance your Mars energy, whether or not this is one of your planets. Use this information and work with Mars to balance, inspire, heal and make magic happen.

POWER COLOUR

RED

Red is evocative and relates to passion, lust, wealth, anger, violence, sex, danger, energy, love and victory. As the colour of blood, it represents physical life.

POWER DAY

TUESDAY

Tyr, the Norse god of war and justice, is the god for whom Tuesday is named (*Tiwesdaeg* being the Anglo-Saxon version). The Romans named the day after Mars, their own god of war, and the Ancient Greeks also named it for their spirit of battle, Ares. Tuesday is a power-through day, and a lot can be achieved with the significant energy of Mars charging you up. With your can-do attitude at the ready, focus on what means most to you and point the full strength of your will directly at that. Concentrate on what lights you up today and nothing can stop you. It's a day for looking after your body temple, so the best day to make appointments for anything medical or health maintaining. Avoid burnout, frustrating people and stressful situations so that you stay on an even keel – Mars can easily fire us up. If you have to compete, Tuesday is the day to come on strong and conquer.

ASTROLOGICAL SIGNS

ARIES AND SCORPIO

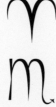

Mars rules Aries and Scorpio (although many modern-day astrologers attribute Scorpio to Pluto).

ELEMENT

FIRE

Fire is the element of Mars, which makes sense when you consider this planet is associated with the hot emotions of passion, lust, competitiveness and anger.

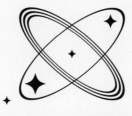

TAROT CARDS

The cards of the Hermit and the Moon are numbered 9 and 18 in the major arcana of the tarot, with 18 becoming 9 when you add 1 + 8. If you are learning tarot or practising readings, understand that these cards are associated with the energy of the number 9 and Mars. They might not seem Mars-like at first glance, but their themes of obtaining power and wisdom, danger, arguments, volatile emotions, following your own path, independence, needing patience, keeping your own counsel and having compassion are truly Martian.

BODY NURTURE ZONES

Mars governs the blood, the immune system (the body's defence force), the muscles and the adrenals (relating to our fight or flight response). When Mars is one of your planets, these health aspects need to be taken care of. Giving your adrenaline a healthy outlet and reducing anything that triggers your fight or flight response is a must, as is keeping your body strong and fit.

✦ ─────────────────────────────────── ✦

ESSENTIAL OILS

Black pepper

Ginger

Clove

Coriander

Bay laurel

The Mars-ruled aromatics are powerful, pungent, energetic and invigorating. They have pain-relieving properties when applied externally. (Be careful, though: they are *strong* and can irritate sensitive skin.) They can be used as inhalants in diffusers or burners for their mood-altering properties, or diluted and applied topically to ease muscular aches and pains.

BLACK PEPPER and GINGER are stimulating and warming, ideal for the burnt-out Mars.

Ginger and CLOVE are both warming, to relieve aching, painful and stiff muscles. (Both must be diluted and never used in the bath.)

CORIANDER and black pepper help if you're feeling stuck and unmotivated or finding it difficult to move forwards. This can happen to Mars types who've been fighting big battles in life.

BAY LAUREL is used for protection and represents victory. It is an uplifting, stimulating tonic.

HEALING HERBS

Cayenne

Ginger

Black pepper

Nettle

Rehmannia

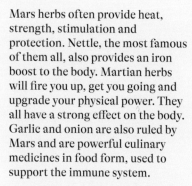

Mars herbs often provide heat, strength, stimulation and protection. Nettle, the most famous of them all, also provides an iron boost to the body. Martian herbs will fire you up, get you going and upgrade your physical power. They all have a strong effect on the body. Garlic and onion are also ruled by Mars and are powerful culinary medicines in food form, used to support the immune system.

CAYENNE is ultra heating, and best used in small amounts on food when you need a little pep in your step. GINGER is also a warmer that can be added to foods or used fresh in a tea. (Note: For Mars people, both should only be used when you are suffering fatigue and need to rekindle your fire.)

BLACK PEPPER adds a touch of Martian heat without being overwhelming (it is often used in protection spells).

NETTLE leaves are rich in iron. This nutritive herb has a lengthy historical use as a blood purifier.

Adrenal fatigue is common for Mars types (who tend to overdo it) and REHMANNIA is a great restorative for this vital gland. It also works on the musculoskeletal system to assist with inflammation.

MAKE SOME MARTIAN MAGIC

Exercise. Get those muscles pumping and that blood flowing. Or, even better, sexercise! (No explanation required.)

Wear red. This colour makes a Mars statement. You will be noticed. You will be heard. You will appear, and feel, strong.

Take action on that daring plan. Today.

Channel some energy into a cause you genuinely care about and get fired up.

FEELING UNBALANCED?

Mars requires movement and abhors stagnation. Move and make moves.

Write yourself a to-do list and feel like a demigod as you tick off those tasks.

Hydrate. Mars is hot and dry, so water will keep the fire in check when you feel overwhelmed and cranky.

NEEDING INSPIRATION?

Tune in to what motivates you and dangle those carrots over your head, so that you can stay on track and feel rewarded for all your hard work.

Do something difficult or a bit daredevil for the sake of the challenge.

Pick a fight that's worth winning – one that provides a beautiful outcome for the greater good.

Get into something competitive to activate your warrior spirit.

MARS MEDITATION

FOR ENERGY

This is an active meditation, perfect for when you need to reset, clear your mind and focus. The Breath of Fire is a yogic classic, designed to feed your flame and energise you. Use this breath meditation whenever your batteries feel a bit flat.

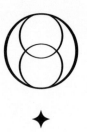

This is a potent breath practice for motivation, strength and personal power. It will provide you with fierce yang energy and bring in Mars support when you need it most. The Breath of Fire is said to balance the blood (ruled by Mars), invigorate the brain and strengthen digestive fire.

Start with thirty seconds at a time; when you are practised and familiar, you can go up to one minute, and then eventually progress to three minutes if you would like. Any longer than three minutes is *much* too much of a good thing. Less is more with this meditation.

If you are prone to dizziness, take it easy, make sure you are seated safely and return to normal breath if you feel lightheaded.

This type of vigorous breathing is not recommended if you are pregnant or menstruating. Instead, try a gentle, modified version. Slow it right down and just breathe evenly, softly and deeply, infusing your body with strength and energy (do not strain, pump your navel or push). A good method is to breathe in for a set count (say four, eight or ten seconds – whatever is comfortable) and out for the same set count. The key is to even out the rhythm of the breath. You will still receive the benefits of the balanced breathing, without overstimulating.

Sit comfortably in a chair with both feet on the ground, or cross-legged on the floor with your upper body straight. (Check your head and neck alignment – it's important not to block the flow by tipping your head forwards or back.)

Rest your hands, with palms facing up or down, on your knees, or bring all the fingertips of your right and left hands together to balance the body.

Gently close your mouth and eyes and take a few normal breaths; focus your mindset on bringing in Mars energy. Breathe in slowly and deeply through the nose, filling from the navel first, all the way up to the lungs. Exhale the breath through the nose from the lungs down to the navel. Do not strain: let the airflow be natural.

Now, inhale and exhale through the nose in short mini breaths, like a dog panting, but through your nose rather than your mouth. Your solar plexus and navel should be gently pumping in rhythm with the breath, and the inhale and exhale should be the same length. The navel goes inwards with the exhale and expands outwards with the inhale. Continue this breath for up to three minutes.

Once the time is up, let your breath go and take a deep inhale and exhale. Open your eyes, sit for a moment to allow the body to adjust, and take a few normal breaths before you slowly get up again.

CREATION ◆ **BEGINNING** ◆ *AMPLIFICATION*

O
✦
V
OI
D

From O we begin, and there is a lot of power in that turning point; O is an empty space, a blank slate, everything and nothing. From nothing always comes something, and this something is full of golden potential. New starts, new beginnings and their accompanying endings are all wrapped up in the personality of this number. That's why its energy represents thresholds and creation. In numerology, O is often overlooked and not considered a true number. What it actually does is provide for regeneration, a starting-over moment and a sense of completion at the same time.

The decades, centuries and millennia feel special and important because of O. They only happen every ten, hundred or thousand years. Which is why we celebrate what we've been through, achieved and experienced at the turn of a new O point. We think of the new decade, century or millennium ahead with a mixture of uncertainty and hope. When we reach milestone decade birthdays, for example, the O energy comes into play and we often want a fresh start to go along with this turning point in life. There is something about a O attached to a number that gives it extra weight. So, for those of you born on the tenth, twentieth or thirtieth of the month, the O magnifies the 1, 2 or 3, making you a super Sun, Moon or Jupiter type. When we use expressions such as 'I've said it a thousand times', 'she's one in a million' or 'this is ten times better', we are emphasising a point. We use numbers with O in them to illustrate our point with extra strength.

O is the Fool in the tarot deck, leaping off a cliff with their past in the background, optimism in their heart and a beginner's mind. The journeys we embark on in life aren't possible without the Os of that first step, the point of creation. When you close one door and open another, you are conspiring with O. Often used to express the absence of something, another point of view about O is the philosophical concept that nature abhors a vacuum and seeks to fill it; therefore, from nothing a new thing is always created. We also have the quantum physics theory of 'no such thing as nothing' – energy can be changed or shifted but never lost. 0 is alchemy in action.

Every ending in your life is a beginning. New phases bring the opportunity to reset and invite in magnificence. 0 moments, such as decade birthdays, or 0 turning points, when you are starting over, are full of creative potential. Even unwanted changes are offering you future wisdom, which is something no amount of money can buy and that can never be taken away. When you begin something, you take a brave leap into the unknown and commune with the fertile spirit of 0. You become a wizard of creativity in your life, shunning passivity and courageously shifting the status quo. Reinventing circumstance and collaborating with creation is a powerful magic. Celebrate 0 points and grab hold of their opportunities. May all of your beginnings become blessings.

O
V
OI
D

THANK YOU ...

For picking up my book and reading to the end.
I hope you found this work illuminating,
uplifting, life affirming and rich in a-ha
moments. Please use the information in this
book to support and enhance the magic and
beauty of who you are. Each number and planet
has its own unique expressions and gifts on
offer, just as every individual person does. Work
with the information that feels right and rings
true for you, discarding whatever doesn't fit.
We all manifest our numbers and planets in
different ways and nothing about this has to
be an inescapable trap. Free will is the most
important aspect of who you are. There is no
such thing as 'one size fits all' with this kind
of wisdom.

With that in mind, please do keep exploring and
learning about numerology as a guidance system
you can play with and use to make the best of
what you've got.

Wishing you all the very best in life,
Jenn

ABOUT THE AUTHOR

Jenn King has revered and studied the bewitching qualities of numbers since childhood. Though she has explored many mystical teachings, the numbers and planets have always reigned supreme.

After more than a decade in the film industry in the UK and Australia, and following a health crisis at age thirty, she decided to change careers and was called back to numerology and planetary wisdom. The innate connection between numbers and planets led her to form her own version of numerology in which each number and its ruling planet come together as one. Since then, she has been writing daily number and planet forecasts and creating personal numerology charts.

Jenn is also a qualified herbalist and aromatherapist, and her love of plants intersects with her love of the planets, as every plant expresses affinity with its own planetary ruler. She frequently advises her numerology clients on compatible herbs and oils to help them better connect with their kindred planets.

WWW.THECOSMICNUMEROLOGIST.COM

IMAGE CREDITS

ACKNOWLEDGEMENTS

This book is dedicated to my mother, who taught me to trust in my magic, to love books and writing, and to follow what matters most to me in life.

To my publisher, Paulina de Laveaux: thank you for believing in me, and for all you have done to give this book the best possible start in life. I am so incredibly grateful and honoured to have you as my publisher. To my brilliant editors, Jane Price and Jessica Levine: thank you for supporting me through this process and for ensuring that every sentence is the best it can possibly be. To my designers extraordinaire, Evi O and Kait Polkinghorne: thank you for your sublime talents and for bringing such perfect beauty to every page. To all at Thames & Hudson: thank you for taking a chance on me, for your unwavering support, and for all your hard work and dedication to bring this book into being.

To my family, who have always loved me unconditionally and encouraged me to follow the paths that sing to me, thank you. To my dad, Adrian: thank you for instilling in me a deep love of numbers and words. To my sister, Fionna, and brothers, Michael and Patrick: you are my true north. Thank you for all that you are.

To all the teachers and healing helpers who have touched my life. Your guidance has been a huge blessing; thank you for all that you do. To Cristina Harris: thank you for always inspiring me with your wise Jupiterian ways. To my dear friends: you know who you are. Thank you for always backing me, believing in, encouraging, supporting and laughing with me. Your friendship means the world.

To my sweet Bailey: thank you for proving unconditional love exists, and for being by my side.

Finally, to the love of my life, David. There are not enough thank yous in the world. You are a priceless gift. You are my greatest teacher. You are the light of my heart.

First published in Australia in 2022
by Thames & Hudson Australia Pty Ltd
11 Central Boulevard, Portside Business Park
Port Melbourne, Victoria 3207
ABN: 72 004 751 964

First published in the United Kingdom in 2022
By Thames & Hudson Ltd
181a High Holborn
London WC1V 7QX

First published in the United States of America in 2022
By Thames & Hudson Inc.
500 Fifth Avenue
New York, New York 10110

Cosmic Numerology © Thames & Hudson Australia 2022

Text © Jenn King

Thames & Hudson Australia wishes to acknowledge that
Aboriginal and Torres Strait Islander people are the first
storytellers of this nation and the traditional custodians of
the land on which we live and work. We acknowledge their
continuing culture and pay respect to Elders past, present
and future.

ISBN 978-1-760-76247-6
ISBN 978-1-760-76289-6 (U.S. edition)

 A catalogue record for this
book is available from the
NATIONAL
LIBRARY National Library of Australia
OF AUSTRALIA

British Library Cataloguing-in-Publication Data
A catalogue record for this book is available from the
British Library

Library of Congress Control Number 2021951346

Every effort has been made to trace accurate ownership of
copyrighted text and visual materials used in this book. Errors
or omissions will be corrected in subsequent editions, provided
notification is sent to the publisher.

Photo: Untitled, Łukasz Łada, 2017

Design: Evi O. Studio | Evi O. & Kait Polkinghorne
Editing: Jane Price
Printed and bound in China by C&C Offset Printing Co., Ltd.

FSC® is dedicated to the promotion of responsible forest
management worldwide. This book is made of material from
FSC®-certified forests and other controlled sources.

Be the first to know about our new releases,
exclusive content and author events by visiting
thamesandhudson.com.au
thamesandhudson.com
thamesandhudsonusa.com

MIX
Paper from
responsible sources
FSC® C008047